The Glory of Man

The Glory of Man

David E. Jenkins

SCM PRESS LTD

334 00542 6

First published 1967
by SCM Press Ltd
26–30 Tottenham Road London N1 4BZ
Third impression 1984

Printed in Great Britain by
Richard Clay (The Chaucer Press) Ltd
Bungay, Suffolk

CONTENTS

PREFACE

THE PURPOSE of the lectures which follow, and which are set out more or less as I delivered them, is to raise a question of truth and to investigate a matter of faith. I wished to put to the test my growing conviction that the two questions 'What is really involved in being a man?' and 'What is truly involved in believing in Jesus Christ?' are inextricably bound up with one another and that both need a great deal of re-thinking.

I have attempted, therefore, to produce a set of lectures which theologically speaking discuss christology, and generally speaking discuss man.

The grounds for continuing to insist in the second half of the twentieth century that humanism inevitably involves theology must be gathered from the lectures themselves. They are designed and intended as an exercise in experimental thinking provoked by data for the status of which I argue as I go along. I do not expect to establish truth. I attempt to report what I believe I have seen, to sketch out what I hope to see, and perhaps to contribute something of weight to be used in the search which we must each one of us make for ourselves.

Both Christians and non-Christians need, I think, to be required pretty sharply to re-consider what they are really talking about in the current debates about God, Jesus, man and the world. The best thing about these debates is that they have ceased to be a matter for experts alone, but they are clearly too serious to be pursued with a sort of slovenly eclecticism. Each man must have broader reasons than his own choice for choosing to enter the debate at the point he does or for pursuing it in the manner he does. Hence I have felt obliged to range as widely as I could and as competently as I could

eclecticism

without obscuring the shape of my argument and my search in the sort of details appropriate to technical discussions between experts in limited fields. And I think it would have hindered rather than helped the purpose with which the lectures were composed had I written them up for publication in a much longer form in which I attempted to bolster their arguments with as much detail as possible. I wish to argue with and on behalf of thinking men in general rather than to pursue scholarly debates.

None the less it would be entirely foreign to the spirit of open and rigorous research which I believe to be demanded in investigating both questions of truth and matters of faith, if I attempted to shelter from detailed criticism by taking refuge in broad arguments. I can scarcely hope that my competence has adequately extended even as far as I have attempted to range in these lectures, and there is clearly need to range much more widely. But what I have said, I have said in the belief that my statement will stand detailed investigation over a wide enough range and at sufficient depth to sustain enough of the argument. While, therefore, I do not address myself to experts, I have no right and no wish to avoid them.

I have added a postscript to the lectures for the reasons stated in it. I am unable to conceive of any present theological or philosophical undertaking as being an end in itself. If it has any validity it must be as a contribution to a continuing enterprise and enquiry. Hence I could not avoid ending the spoken lectures with a question mark and the published version with a postscript designed as a preface to something further. I hope that the lectures sufficiently reflect my conviction that neither in theory nor in practice should there be any conflict between absolute commitment to Jesus Christ and complete openness to the future.

EXTRACT

FROM THE LAST WILL AND TESTAMENT

OF THE LATE

REV. JOHN BAMPTON

Canon of Salisbury

'. . . I give and bequeath my Lands and Estates to the Chancellor, Masters, and Scholars of the University of Oxford for ever, to have and to hold all and singular the said Lands or Estates upon trust, and to the intents and purposes hereinafter mentioned; that is to say, I will and appoint that the Vice-Chancellor of the University of Oxford for the time being shall take and receive all the rents, issues, and profits thereof, and (after all taxes, reparations, and necessary deductions made) that he pay all the remainder to the endowment of eight Divinity Lecture Sermons, to be established for ever in the said University, and to be performed in the following:

'I direct and appoint, that, upon the first Tuesday in Easter Term, a Lecturer be yearly chosen by the Heads of Colleges only, and by no others, in the room adjoining to the Printing-House, between the hours of ten in the morning and two in the afternoon, to preach eight Divinity Lecture Sermons, the year following, at St. Mary's in Oxford, between the commencement of the last month in Lent Term, and the end of the third week in Act Term.

'Also I direct and appoint, that the eight Divinity Lecture Sermons shall be preached upon either of the following Subjects—to conform and establish the Christian Faith, and to confute all heretics and schismatics—upon the divine authority of the holy Scriptures— upon the authority of the writings of the primitive Fathers, as to the faith and practice of the primitive Church—upon the Divinity of our Lord and Saviour Jesus Christ—upon the Divinity of the Holy Ghost—upon the Articles of the Christian Faith, as comprehended in the Apostles' and Nicene Creeds.

'Also I direct, that thirty copies of the eight Divinity Lecture Sermons shall be always printed, within two months after they are preached; and one copy shall be given to the Chancellor of the University, and one copy to the Head of every College, and one copy to the Mayor of the city of Oxford, and one copy to be put into the Bodleian Library; and the expense of printing them shall be paid out of the revenue of the Land or Estates given for establishing the Divinity Lecture Sermons; and the Preacher shall not be paid nor be entitled to the revenue, before they are printed.

'Also I direct and appoint, that no person shall be qualified to preach the Divinity Lecture Sermons, unless he has taken the degree of Master of Arts at least, in one of the two Universities of Oxford or Cambridge; and that the same person shall never preach the Divinity Lecture Sermons twice.'

I

Our Concern

THE BAMPTON LECTURES of 1866 were delivered by the Reverend Henry Parry Liddon, student of Christ Church. They were entitled *The Divinity of Our Lord and Saviour Jesus Christ*. In his summing up towards the end of his eighth lecture, Liddon said: 'The doctrine of Christ's Divinity does not merely bind us to the historic past, and above all to the first records of Christianity; it is at this hour the strength of the Christian Church. There are forces abroad in the world of thought which, if viewed by themselves, might well make a Christian fear for the future of Christendom and of humanity. It is not merely that the Church is threatened with the loss of possessions secured to her by the reverence of centuries, and of a place of honour which has perhaps guarded civilization more effectively than it has strengthened religion. The Church has once triumphed without these gifts of Providence, and, if God wills, she can again dispense with them. But never since the first years of the Gospel was fundamental Christian truth denied and denounced so largely with such passionate animosity, as is the case at this moment in each of the most civilized nations of Europe.' (pp. 746f.)

Now, after one hundred further years of the Debate about God and Christianity, passionate animosity to fundamental Christian truth is not our immediate and obvious problem. Rather we would seem to be faced with a good deal of uncertainty as to what fundamental Christian truth is. In particular, not all Christians would themselves seem to be prepared to agree with Liddon that, 'The doctrine of Christ's Divinity . . . is at this hour the strength of the Christian Church.' Perhaps, therefore, we should proceed to inquire what is at this hour the strength of the Christian Church. But we cannot really start here, for the real question pressed upon us at and by the present time is not 'What is the strength of the Christian Church?' at all. The real, pressing and timely question is 'Why give any time or thought to enquiring into what is or was or might be the strength of the Christian Church?'

In 1866 Liddon saw the Church threatened with loss of possessions, reverence and a place of honour, although he did not see this threat as necessarily hurtful—indeed, he hints that it might well be liberating. Today, one hundred years later, the Church of England has certainly still not lost all possessions and still retains at least formally not a few places of honour. In the University of Oxford, for example, the statutes continue to require regular University sermons marked as formal and honourable acts of the University by the presence of the Vice Chancellor and Proctors. But all this sort of thing presents the appearance much more of a survival of something that was honourable and powerful in the past rather than the presence of something that is generally relevant now and vital for the future. It would be unrealistic as things are today to start an investigation into what may be held to be the fundamental truth of Christianity and into what may be claimed as the real strength of the Christian Church with the unexamined presupposition that such an enquiry is, of course, worthwhile. We must rather ask why we should now be concerned with an investigation into the truths asserted as part of Christianity, the doctrines put forward by the Christian Church, the claims of divinity for Jesus Christ, or, indeed, with any of the things concerning Jesus. What grounds are there for claiming that such concerns should be the concern of men and women in general?

I assume one ground which I take to be self-evident, universal and inescapable. I assume that our concern is with persons. If it is not, then I assert that our concern *ought* to be with persons. To refuse or ignore this concern is a failure to face up to what is involved in being a human being. To reject a concern with persons which is commensurate with the concern which persons as such demand is a refusal to face facts which amounts to a fundamental error of judgement about value. It is also a rejection of value, an attitude of immorality, which flies in the face of recognizable facts. People who refuse a proper concern for persons are immoral as human beings and wrong as judges of matters of fact.

If a man refuses to be concerned with persons in a manner which seeks to respond properly to the fact that they are persons, then he is refusing to face up to reality. By this I mean that he is failing to take account both of what is really the case and of what really matters in the case as it is. It is for this reason that I assert that our concern ought to be with persons. This assertion is not merely commending a possible attitude or describing an optional concern. It is saying that whatever concerns people may in fact show themselves to have by the ways in which they occupy their lives, none the less every human being is under a compulsion, *both factual and moral*, to be concerned with persons.

At least two apparently rash and currently unfashionable claims are contained in or implied by such a statement of concern. The first is that it is possible with reason and persuasiveness to demand general assent to a universal truth of some significance about human beings as such. The most prevalent current presupposition would seem to be that it is possible at most to make limited generalizations about recognizably limited groups of human beings from limited stand-points, such as those of biology or sociology or psychology. And that when we get on to claims about values no universal statements are permissible at all. The second difficult claim is that values are inherently present in facts or that there are some matters of fact (in this case—what is in fact involved in being a person) which demand a certain evaluation because of their inherent observable nature. Difficult and awkward as these claims are, I make them deliberately and unhesitatingly, for they seem to me to be plainly involved in this concern with persons and for persons which I find as an inescapable and demanding feature of my living and which I put forward as an inescapable demand on the living of every man and woman.

But what is this inherent observable nature of what is in fact involved in being a person, which calls for the sort of claim I am attempting to establish? You must look and see. You must consider in what ways it matters to you to be you, keeping your investigation in the first person. What does it mean to me to be me and what could I wish it to mean? You must also reflect on what you regard as your own best and most worthwhile relations with others. You must further consider what you know or believe to be your own best wishes and hopes for those particular persons whom you care for most. If you will attend to yourself in relation to these other individuals who matter to you and to others who matter to you in relation to yourself, then you will have some idea of what is involved in being a person.

At least you will have the opportunity of forming some such idea. You may find that you do not have the courage or the will to let this idea of what is involved in being a person come to any clarity in your consideration and awareness. But this will be so, if it is so, precisely because what is involved in being a person is intrinsically and self-authenticatingly valuable. And that which is valuable and seen to be so is, as such, a source of demand or claim upon us. It may be, therefore, that we refuse to admit any clear recognition of what is involved in being a person because we wish to reject the claims which being a person in relation to persons makes upon us. If this is your case, then in your very refusal to admit any understanding of what I am talking about in claiming a universal concern for persons there is contained some understanding of that claim and its justness.

It may be, on the other hand, that all this talk about concern for persons seems exaggerated and sentimental. We may all of us be moved to think at some time in our lives that being a person and being in relation to persons is of supreme importance. But to claim that a concern for persons as persons is, and must be, the central and universal ground for our approach to life is to fail to recognize the way in which so much in human affairs distorts and frustrates the development of persons. In particular, it is to ignore that there are good grounds for holding that each and every human being has built in as part of his or her personality elements which work against the production of a rounded and fulfilled personalness—either in the individual as a person or in those other persons with whom the individual has to do. But here I would seek to call attention to what I would describe as the dimension, or perhaps the scale, of the frustration of personalness. It is a dimension which is tellingly illus-

trated in the literature of the Absurd or in the theatr
Indifference, and not infrequently experienced in cy
suality. All these and other forms of human reacti
involved in being human can be reasonably and pow
evidence of what is inherently involved in being a person, and of the
value of being a person, even if the value is glimpsed only in the
moment of its extinction or seen through the tragedy of its frustration. Thus I expect agreement to the claim that our concern is or
must be with persons, on the ground that reflection will intuitively
show the strength of this claim. Further, the claim stands even if the
intuition is inhibited from its full force by a fear of what that claim,
if acknowledged, would involve for him who acknowledges it. It
stands also, even if the intuition is threatened with nullity by the
attacks and frustration to which persons are in fact often subjected.
We can still see that our concern is, or ought to be, with persons.

But can we maintain this despite the fact that we cannot define
precisely what is meant by 'being a person'? By referring you to
your awareness of yourself and of what it is to be an 'I', and by
asking you to reflect on your relationships with those fellow human
beings who matter to you most, I have been seeking to provide you
with an ostensive definition of 'being a person', I have been trying to
point to what is meant and indicated, although it cannot be defined.
In an attempt at definition we might be inclined to say that an
essential feature of being a person is a capacity to enter into, and to
appreciate, reciprocal and reciprocated relationships with other
human beings. But I suspect that a definition of this nature would
turn out to have at least some element of circularity in it. For the
relationships in question have to be *personal* ones, and not just any
instances whatever of relatedness between human beings. A personal
relationship is one which does justice to something peculiarly human
and peculiarly worthwhile among the potentialities of our existence
as men. Once one has experienced it, one can tell the difference
between being treated as a person and being treated impersonally or
as less than a human self. But the possibilities involved in being a
person cannot be made clear from theory alone or learned from a
definition. Moreover, it is clear that some human beings, never
having been treated as persons, do not know what it is to be a person.

ınd we who, I continue to claim, do know something of what is involved in being a person, have not learnt this from our general relations with all the human beings with whom we have had dealings, nor do we easily regard every human being as such, as a person. Further, many of our casual dealings which involve other human beings are not, and probably neither can be nor need to be, personal dealings. The quality and possibility of 'personalness', if I may so put it, is something which is learnt from some particular relationships with some few human beings who treat us as persons. Thus it turns out that this universal concern for persons as persons which I am putting forward as a common and acceptable basis for our investigation into the possible strength of Christianity is neither definable nor a universal feature of the experience human beings have of one another. Rather it is learnt from certain particular relationships, and can be pointed to as an experienced reality and possibility of singular importance.

It must certainly be acknowledged that this overriding concern for persons is, looked at from some points of view, of precarious status. If it is not fully definable, or definable only in a circular way, then it is particularly vulnerable to dismissal by the narrowly matter-of-fact approach of so much current thought. It is, moreover, all the more vulnerable in that there are currently available various plausible and allegedly scientific forms of *reductionism* which can be drawn, for example, from the biological or psychological or social sciences or from combinations of them. What I have in mind are the various and repeated attempts made to show that the features of truly human living—personality, love, the awareness and pursuit of value and the like—are, in the last analysis, *nothing but* particular combinations of entities, forces and relationships which can be exhaustively studied and defined by the sciences in question as their techniques and information become progressively more refined. The strength of one or more of these cases for reducing the phenomena of human personality to realities which are the proper subject matter of a necessarily deterministic science is well known. Therefore, in seeking to take as an agreed starting point a concern for persons as persons, I am asking for the acceptance as real and compelling of something which I admit to being not satisfactorily definable and which I acknowledge to be subject to the dissolving analysis of a great deal of weighty scientific thinking and knowledge.

Finally, if we are realistically to sustain this starting point, we must be aware that this concern for persons is not only threatened by the vagueness of indefinability and undermined by possible scientific forms of reductionism. Its existence as a matter of fundamental importance and reality is repeatedly contradicted in all human experience. It is scarcely our experience that most people most of the time are concerned to treat one another as persons in any deep or significant sense.

None the less, I continue to claim that our concern is and must be with persons. This is so because among all the uncertainties of definition, the possibilities of reductionism and the experiences of contradiction, we are able, in and through some of our relationships with some human beings, to perceive a fact and glimpse a value, or possibly, to perceive a value and glimpse a fact. This coincidence— or is it identity?—of fact and value is observed and experienced by us in the case of one or two of those empirical entities of animated flesh and blood who are known generically as human beings, but who are particularly known to us as persons with proper names of their own. He or she, father or mother, sister or brother, husband or wife, child or friend, simply exists as a particular piece of givenness. He or she is a fact. But the fact is that *this* he or she, precisely because he or she exists in his or her own particular and personal way, has a unique, intrinsic and demanding value. But this value *consists* in the fact that he or she exists as his or her own particular and personal self. It is thus, when we know some people as persons, that we are able to perceive that in persons, fact and value, existence and worth-whileness, coincide. And in perceiving this fact, which is the valuable existence of a person, we are at the same time confronted with the fact that our concern is with persons. To see what is involved in being a person is to know that here lies an inescapable concern.

But we have not even yet dealt sufficiently with the fact that this concern, although inescapable, is both unclear and precarious. We know, or can know, that because of what is involved in being a person our concern is and must be with persons. But we are not clear just what it is that is involved in being a person, nor are we clear that we are able or willing to pursue that concern properly. In this situation of uncertainty and precariousness the important point would seem to be this. We have some understanding of what it is or might be to be a person. This is sufficient to show us that in our awareness of 'personalness' we are catching glimpses of a reality which demands investigation. The demand for investigation has force in a twofold way. It is the demand of a given fact for explanation and the demand of a seen value for commitment and response. Thus in our perception of 'personalness' we are confronted with a coincidence of fact and value which shows every sign of being an identity and which requires an investigation and response proper to the reality which is perceived. It is on grounds such as these that I maintain, as I have already said (p. 3), that: 'If a man refuses to be concerned with persons in a manner which seeks to respond properly to the fact that they are persons, then he is refusing to face up to reality'. And I hope it is now clearer why I went on to say: 'By this I mean that he is failing to take account both of what is really the case and of what really matters in the case as it is'. I propose no theory and require no prior acceptance of a theory as our starting point for an investigation into the question of the strength of Christianity. I simply direct attention to the existence of our concern for persons and to the observable nature of that concern, and I insist that the existence and reality of this concern for persons is quite as much a fact to be reckoned with as are the uncertainties and precariousness to which I have also referred.

Thus I am seeking to avoid anything theoretical, and to do without any presupposed theory in looking for a reasonable and agreed starting point from which we may consider whether we should pay any attention to claims made for, and statements made about, Jesus. I think this is necessary because in our present circumstances we clearly cannot assume any widely agreed metaphysical presuppositions. But although I am trying to avoid metaphysical presuppositions, I cannot avoid raising metaphysical questions. Indeed, I am being highly metaphysical. For I am raising questions about, and seeking at least limited agreement about, what counts as 'real'. That is to say that I am asking you to consider what features of your own and other people's experience you ought to count as most weighty, as most worthy of your faith and commitment, in deciding what is really the case and what really matters in the case as it is. And my argument is that in our concern for persons we can see that we are on to an area of experienced reality which has strong claims to be treated as definitive for our decisions as reasonable human beings about what is to be counted as reality. And in so arguing I am also insisting that our decision about what is to be counted as reality must be related to both what is observed to be the case and what is judged to be worthwhile in, or in relation to, what is observed. I cannot accept the position that in the last human analysis it does not matter what is there or what is observable but that what matters is our attitude towards 'it', whatever 'it' is. To dissociate judgements of reality (= judgements about existence, about what is really there) from judgements of reality (= judgements about value, about what really matters) seems to me to be the way of withdrawal, immaturity and, in the end, madness. The fundamental question is 'What *is* there?', and *then* 'How worthwhile is it?'. And I focus attention on our concern for persons because here we are able to be aware, with more or less clarity, of the force of an area in which existence and value seem to be strongly and factually linked. There is, therefore, a very strong *prima facie* case for looking at this area of 'personalness' to which we are alerted by our concern for persons as the starting point for any investigation into any subject matter which claims to be of particular significance for us as human beings.

It is necessary to discuss and explain this at some length, as the too-ready adoption of slogans like 'Persons matter', or even 'Love is the only thing that matters', usually leads to, if it does not already stem from, sentimentality. Sentimentality is clearly worse than useless in any attempt to face up to and assess reality, for sentimentality is the determination to obscure reality in the haze of feelings which we find comfortable. For any serious investigation some much more rigorously established starting point is required. If, then, we are to start from our concern for persons, as I believe we should, we must take considerable pains to establish what it is we are talking about and where we are starting from. Since, also, we are raising questions about what is to be judged to be real we cannot avoid facing questions about the definition of 'personalness' (what is involved in this area).

We have to be concerned with claims to reduce the alleged facts of personalness to the observed facts of science. And we have to face experience which could be against personalness.

Finally, therefore, let us see where we have got to in setting forth and investigating the claim that our primary concern is, and ought to be, with persons. I have attempted to get you to see that we have a sufficient idea of what is involved in being a person and of the sort of concern which is a concern for persons. But we must also be prepared to say that there is a sense in which we do not know what is involved in being a person. Thus, we do not know how far being a person goes. That is to say we do not know what, if anything, could be properly described as the fulfilment of being a person, what are the possibilities as yet latent in human personalness, and what are all the demands which would have to be made on, and met by, men and women as persons, if men and women are to be truly and fully persons. Nor do we know what is the relation of the reality involved in being a person to other realities which we observe or encounter in the universe and in human life. Here we return to the possible reductionisms of science and the experienced contradictions of living already referred to. These possibilities and these experiences present us, as I have already suggested, with claims to reality which have to be evaluated in relation to the reality experienced through our awareness of the concern for persons.

So we have our concern for persons presenting us with the demands of a fact which is intrinsically valuable. But we do not know the full nature of the fact or the full weight of the value. Moreover, the status of the fact and the extent of the possibilities inherent in the value are threatened on two fronts. There is the claim that the facts involved in the field of personalness ought to be reduced to that type of data which is the proper subject matter of scientifically deterministic procedures. And there is the assertion that the values involved in being a person cannot survive the actual contradictions inflicted on personalness by the hard facts of the processes of the universe and of the actualities of human living.

The mystery of the fact of being a person, it is claimed, is to be reduced to the facts of the appropriate sciences. The mystery of the value of being a person, it is asserted, will succumb to the indifferent realities both of the universe as process and of human life as actually lived. And what in any case is the nature and extent of the mystery of being a person?

Let us be quite clear that to focus attention on what is involved in being a person is to raise a question quite as much as to point to a fact. But this is simply to increase our awareness of the dimensions of our concern for persons. In this concern we are made vividly aware of an area of human living, of experienced reality, which demands our investigation and commitment—investigation through commitment and commitment opening up further possibilities of investigation. In fact our experience of personalness invites us to faith, a faith which is to be put to the test of investigation and action. In our experience of what is involved in being a person in relation to other persons, we catch glimpses of a possible reality which is self-evidently worthwhile. Let us therefore see if this glimpsed reality of personalness will stand up to the threatened realities of actual human life and the observed processes of the universe. It is surely most reasonable, most valuable, most existential and most human, to put our faith in the possibilities of personalness. At any rate it is a faith which we have very strong grounds for trying out.

If there are those who have no glimmering of faith in the possibilities of personalness and no inkling of a desire to consider the possible kindling of such a faith, then with such I have, in the course of these lectures, little hope of communication. For my concern with Jesus Christ is linked in the closest possible way with *our* concern for persons. I am inviting you to undertake with me an investigation which I believe to be scientific in method, faithful in mood and human in its bearing. Two things strike me. I find myself confronted with two areas in which I believe I see particularly significant and demanding data. The first area is the area of our concern for persons. The second area is that of the things concerning Jesus. Of the first area I have sought to speak in this first lecture. The rest of the lectures are concerned with the second area and with the interaction between what is involved in our concern for persons and what is involved in the things concerning Jesus. I hope that the investigation contained in the lectures as a whole will give some demonstration that I am justified in the close linking which I find between our concern for persons and the things concerning Jesus.

I believe that the investigation to which I invite you is scientific in method, because it can be sufficiently shown that both in the area of our concern for persons and in the area of the things concerning Jesus we are confronted with data which has a *prima facie* claim to be considered as real and to be relevant to our assessment of reality. Hence we are fully entitled to investigate carefully what sort of data this can reasonably be claimed to be, and what bearing it can be said to have. We do not start from presuppositions or from theories but from what we believe to be given us, data, that which strikes us in our concern for persons and in the things concerning Jesus. The investigation is faithful in mood because, as I have sought to show, the data presented to us does seem to involve an intermingling of fact and value. Hence we are all the time concerned with that which at least looks as if it demands not merely investigation but commit-ment. We are investigating areas which on mere inspection can be seen to be important to us as human beings, or which at least look as if they would be important if they should turn out to be able to stand up to tests of reality. Hence they invite faith, commitment to them as real, to see if they turn out to be as real as they appear to be or as real as we would hope them to be. The way in which the investigation is human in its bearing can emerge only as it proceeds.

Hence I invite you to look at some of the things concerning Jesus, to see how far those things are related to our concern for persons. I believe that it will appear that the things concerning Jesus not only clearly tie in with our concern for persons, but have a defining and validating relevance. That is to say, that the things concerning Jesus both show us the direction in which lies the true fulfilment of the possibility and mystery of personalness, and then assure us that the fulfilment is a real possibility and promise, to be established in its reality over against, and in relation to, all the asserted realities of human life and the processes of the universe. If our concern is with persons, then Jesus is our concern.

II

Concern with Persons and Concern with Jesus

WE ARE NOW to investigate some of the things concerning Jesus with a view to demonstrating the interaction between these things and our concern for persons. As I have already said, the cumulative effect of the argument of the whole of the lectures is put forward as justifying the claim that this interaction is highly significant, indeed definitive, for our understanding of persons and of the world. But before we can proceed further in our overall inquiry, it is clearly necessary to give some account of why I select the particular things concerning Jesus that I do and to give some indication of what the status of these 'things' is. That is to say, I must first of all explain my decision to focus attention on the assertions made about, and the claims made for, Jesus which I am about to discuss. Then, secondly, I must give my grounds for holding that the assertions and claims under discussion can either be, or point towards, data which is relevant and weighty for determining the status of our concern for persons now. This is clearly necessary, as I am drawing material for this and the next two lectures from certain developments in Christian thinking about Jesus which took place in the first five centuries of the existence of Christianity and the Christian Church. Why then do I select what I do within that period, and how can I maintain that thinking within that period which is so remote from ours, not so much in time as in its whole manner of looking at the world, is of weight for us now?

I am going to discuss and make use of three types of statement made about Jesus or claimed to be based on things about Jesus. The first type comprises those which make use of various facets of thought about the Logos current in the first three centuries of the Christian era to make statements about the universal significance of Jesus. Then I shall turn to the implications of the discussion about the status of Jesus which took place in the fourth century in connection with the teaching of Arius and the Arians. Finally, I shall be considering the fifth century discussion in the Church about the relation of the divine in Jesus to the human in him. Clearly the topics chosen are a specialized selection from all the possible topics about Jesus which might be considered. Equally clearly, I shall be highly selective even within the material of the selected topics themselves. So it is very necessary to make clear my criteria of selection. It is quite simple. I have chosen those features of those topics within the sum total of the things concerning Jesus which appear to me to be most directly relevant to our current concerns and our current predicament with regard to persons and the significance of personalness. As I discuss the material, I shall endeavour to give some hints of the bearing which it has on this concern and this predicament. But it will not be until the second half of the lectures that I shall seek to demonstrate clearly what this bearing is. Thus, at this stage, I can only declare my criterion and explain the principle of my working method. Whether the criterion has been properly applied and whether the method leads to any positive results can appear only as the whole argument proceeds.

This matter of the working method is most important. It is necessary to make it clear that I am asking for a sustained effort in experimental thinking and I am directing attention to some examples of earlier experimental thinking which I believe I can show to be helpful and important to us now in the sort of thinking which we are compelled to do, and which we would wish to do, about persons. I direct attention back to earlier experimental thinking arising out of the things concerning Jesus because I believe that we shall find help here in our task of deciding what now we are to find 'thinkable' about the world, about ourselves, about personalness. I see no reason to succumb to the insidious plea that we must think what is 'thinkable'. Rather I retain the belief that one of the challenges of being a human being is that we are faced with the opportunity of deciding what we ought to think. If men had accepted what their generation found thinkable, we should have had no science and precious little humanness. Nor do I see why we should succumb to the arrogant complacency of assuming that what we may call 'the modern world-view' is a final and decisive arbiter of what we, as men and human beings, can or ought to think. When it comes to attempting to decide what and how we ought, responsibly and humanly, to think, there is more data than that which counts as data on some understandings of the scientific method. At least that is my contention, and I am issuing an invitation to join with me in putting this contention to the test. But I must stress that this does call for a 'sustained effort in experimental thinking' and I am aware that readiness to enter on such a sustained effort calls in itself for an act of faith.

The act of faith called for is not a consciously or explicitly Christian one. It simply involves readiness to believe that there are areas of human experience and avenues of human knowing which are worth exploring with openness, perseverance and hope. We do not have to know in advance what we are to be open to, nor what we are persevering for, nor what we have hope of. But we have to believe that openness, perseverance and hope are proper and, indeed, demanding possibilities for human beings, and we have to act on this belief. Such action will demand patience. We shall have to be patient in pursuing investigations far enough to allow the course of the investigation to disclose whether or not it is fruitful. We must not impatiently foreclose an avenue of investigation by premature and *a priori* decisions that it cannot be 'relevant' or that it demands an attitude of mind which is 'unthinkable'. We are engaged in inquiring how we should think, and what is given to us that is relevant to us, and what that relevance means for us. We are, in fact, refusing to believe, until we are compelled to believe it, that human beings are inevitably shut up within any concept of what is 'thinkable' or what is 'relevant' whatever.

I have, therefore, selected the particular things concerning Jesus which I have, precisely because I believe it can be shown that they both strengthen and inform this belief in the open possibilities which are involved in being a human being. The selection of data which is believed to be relevant to the hypothesis which one hopes to establish is, surely, a permissible, indeed a necessary, part of any valid experimental investigation. It is, however, necessary to labour this point in connection with our own particular investigation, because in what would be more normally called a scientific investigation, it would by no means be so evident that faith of some sort, perhaps of various sorts, was presupposed. In fact, the most rigorous of scientific investigations is based on presuppositions which involve faith both in the sense of an unproved decision about the way things really are and in the sense of a commitment to try out that decision in practice. But we are not here concerned to pursue further the question of the true basis of the scientific method and its presuppositions. What I am concerned to establish here is that it must not be pre-judged that my decision to select our concern with personalness and then to select certain topics within what I am calling 'the things concerning Jesus' and to juxtapose these two sets of selected material is itself nothing but prejudice.

My selection certainly involves faith in the possibilities of personalness *and* faith in the significance of the things concerning Jesus. But I have tried to show in the first lecture that faith in the possibilities of personalness is based on a reasonable judgement and is a worthwhile commitment. I am hoping to go on to show in the rest of the lectures that faith in the things concerning Jesus is at least reasonable and worthwhile in the same sense. And I am now engaged in arguing that setting up and carrying out an investigation which involves faith as a presupposition is not inevitably a prejudiced operation but is indeed the only way of proceeding with any sort of valid investigation at all. You have to believe that the area which you are investigating is worth investigating. Only the investigation itself will show whether this is so, i.e. whether your faith is strengthened, redirected or destroyed.

Further, this particular investigation is a particularly delicate and complex one because it involves questions about the fundamental nature of, and possibilities in, human life and the universe at large. Perhaps one needs a great deal of faith, which will seem to some people overwhelming stupidity, to undertake such an investigation at all. For the investigation raises questions about what is really real, what is truly true, what counts as data and what the data is good for. Some people hold that such questions cannot be proper questions. To them one must say that the investigation is precisely about whether they are proper questions or not, for the investigation is concerned with inquiring into whether we have evidence to help us in answering such questions. In fact the whole laborious paraphernalia of these lectures so far, with their tiresome refusal to get on with anything, is designed to show that the question of what is a proper question must be kept open to investigation. Or to put the matter less linguistically and more obviously metaphysically, I have been concerned to argue that it is neither scientific nor human to decide in advance where reality and value truly lie, nor to accept uncritically any presuppositions about what is thinkable as having closed the question of the limits within which we may properly think.

It should not occasion surprise that the opening lectures of what is formally a course of lectures on christology should be given over to discussion of methods of investigation and that this discussion should reveal that what is involved is an investigation into our understanding of such difficult and slippery concepts as reality, truth, humanity, personalness. For the scandal of the Christian claim (which Christians at any rate in earlier ages have believed to be the glory of the Christian gospel) has been that it has been asserted that at the heart of the things concerning Jesus there is the truth which is Jesus, and that this truth is declaratory of, and definitive of, what is lasting in reality, what is fully worthwhile in value, what is abiding in truth, what is possible for humanity and what is fulfillable in personalness. But we cannot in our present climate of opinion argue about this directly because we are prevented from getting to the scandal that such a claim should be made, or such a gospel preached *about Jesus*, rather than about some other person or some other philosophy. For it is a much more immediate scandal in most of our modern thinking that one should claim to be able, still more to be obliged, to speak at all about such things as abiding reality, ultimate value, or the fulfilment of personalness.

Therefore, I have to make it clear that I know that I am making what may well appear to be an arbitrary selection of material from an unpromising field in order to tackle questions which may well be thought to be either nonsensical or not able to be answered. I hope that the foregoing argument has sufficiently shown my grounds for proceeding in this manner. My further hope is that the subsequent argument will show that the undertaking is neither as nonsensical nor as impracticable as it may seem. I shall return in Lectures V and VI to this question of presuppositions about our understanding of reality as a whole, and there demonstrate that we cannot escape questions about what is universally valid or significant, i.e. questions about the nature of reality. I shall then direct your attention to the fact that one's presuppositions or decisions about the nature of reality practically affect one's existential and immediate approach to the situations and problems involved in being human. And I shall show conversely that one's existential approach to being human implies a judgement about the 'real nature of things'. In other words, I shall argue that the history of ideas makes it clear that we cannot escape taking or implying a universal view of things and that it is sheer escapism to pretend otherwise. This argument will reinforce my case for having considered in the first place the possible universal significance of the concern for persons, and for directing your attention to areas in the things concerning Jesus which have to do with the universal significance of Jesus.

But having explained my method and criterion of selection, as the best way of giving them a working justification, I have still to put forward my grounds for holding even experimentally and tentatively that among the things concerning Jesus discussed and asserted in the first five centuries of the Christian Church there can be that which will be useful to us now as data in deciding what is thinkable about man, the world and reality. Here again my answer can be partial only. What I have to do is to explain why I have a case for starting from where I do. Whether I turn out to have made a false start or not can appear only from the course and completion of the whole investigation. I hold that the discussions concerning Jesus in the first five Christian centuries may well provide data for guiding us in our present judgements for the following reasons.

It can be shown that the questions which were then discussed in terms of the things concerning Jesus are the same questions as now

confront us, about how we are to understand our human existence
in the face of the processes of the universe and in the face of what
actually happens in human lives, both individually and corporately.
It can at least do us no harm to consider what predecessors of ours,
under conditions very different from ours, made of these questions.
The very difference of their view-point might provide some stimulating, and possibly corrective, cross-checking on the way we now look
at these questions, and so help us to escape from complete abandon-
ment to subjectivism and relativism.

Further, we are surely entitled to ask ourselves whether our own
whole way of looking at things has not settled down into a mythology,
an accepted frame of ideas, a taken-for-granted way of looking
which is, in its own way, as limited and as limiting as those frames of
reference which we have now become accustomed to refer to as the
mythology of earlier ages. Why not, therefore, challenge one mythology with another, i.e. confront the assumptions of the twentieth
century with the formulations of the first to the fifth, when it can be
shown that both are concerned with the same human questions?
This would seem the more likely to be a fruitful confrontation if it
should turn out to be the case that on the one hand, the formulations
of the early centuries contain the germs both of our concern for
personalness and of much of our scientific approach to the universe,
while on the other, our twentieth-century assumptions are permitting
personalness and humanness to be placed in jeopardy. It will be the
task of lectures V and VI to argue this latter point, after, I hope,
lectures III and IV have established the former.

But the nub of the case for pressing this investigation with
material drawn from the first five Christian centuries is that the
topics we shall consider demonstrate the dominating influence in
those centuries of the things concerning Jesus, and therefore bear
witness to the creative impact of Jesus on the thought and human
understanding of that time. We shall be considering how men felt
obliged to understand their life in the world and in the universe in
which they lived, as a result of their acceptance of certain things
concerning Jesus as decisive data. The case for taking their thought
seriously, and investigating the possible interaction between their
thought and ours, lies here. They acted and investigated on the

faithful assumption and commitment that Jesus was a given focus and source of material for forming their views about human life and for directing their responses to, and actions in, the situation of human living. They acted on the assumption that in, and in connection with, Jesus they had data of decisive importance about the true facts and the real values of human life. What I wish to do is to investigate the nature, the basis and the bearing of this understanding.

I claim that this is an interesting thing to do in any case because a confrontation of two worked-out mythologies through some consideration of their working-out may well prove fruitful. I suggest further that it may well prove an urgently desirable thing to do in view of the fact that certain understandings of personalness and humanity which arose out of, and in connection with, the assumptions about Jesus are now threatened. And I argue still further that those assumptions of the early Christian thinkers have a claim upon the consideration of any man who has a mind which is humanly and scientifically open to the possibilities of significant evidence arising anywhere out of the givenness either of the universe or of history.

This claim arises because the basis of the dominating influence of the things concerning Jesus in the period we have to consider was held to lie in the fact that the creative impact of Jesus arose out of his historical existence and rôle. We are not dealing with cosmic and anthropological speculations which take in Jesus, we are confronted with beliefs about the world and man *based on Jesus*. At least that is the claim built into the experimental thinking which we are to study. And that is the main interest of this thinking for me, and the reason why I juxtapose it with our concern for persons as a possible source of data for our understanding of human life in the universe.

For I believe this thinking can be shown to be truly experimental thinking in that the conclusions reached or the faith held concerning man, the world and God was never determined by what the Christian thinkers had hitherto found 'thinkable'. Rather they allowed the theories which they had taken for granted as established in the thinking of the non-Christian world to be challenged, corrected and even in some way determined by what they held to be the truth of the things concerning Jesus. Thus they treated these things concerning Jesus as highly significant experimental data and this they did because they believed that at least the basis of the things concerning Jesus had been given in history in the actual life and rôle of Jesus.

In investigating our concern for persons we find that we are confronted with a given reality or given realities which have weight enough to challenge any theory which pretends to delimit for us what is 'thinkable' or to determine for us how we are to understand the universe and our place in it. This is the argument of my first lecture and it may be put in the form of the question, 'Why should we allow anything other than that which we perceive in, and experience through, our concern for persons to determine our understanding of reality, in the sense both of that which is in fact the case and in the sense of that which is truly worthwhile?' As we consider *this* question, then, I suggest that we should also consider how the things concerning Jesus were understood by the Christians of the early centuries to work in exactly the same way. That is to say, they received the things concerning Jesus as likewise weighty enough both in their factual status and in their value demand to require them to treat that which was given in connection with Jesus as determining data for their understanding of the total context of their living in the universe—of which one feature was that Jesus had lived and played a certain rôle in it. I am trying the experiment of juxtaposing the *prima facie* claim to universal significance exposed through our concern for persons with the historically made claim for the universal significance of Jesus. This I do because I believe it to be the case that our present comprehension of the concern for persons received its initial shaping from the Christian understanding of the universal significance of Jesus. I further believe it to be the case that it is a proper and renewed understanding of the universal significance of Jesus which saves and fulfils our concern for persons. And I am attempting the experiment of these lectures to see if this can, indeed, be shown.

But before I can proceed to the examination of the early experimental thinking I must endeavour by way of conclusion to this lecture to clarify what I mean by, for example, talking of 'that which was given in connection with Jesus' or by making claims based on the life and rôle of Jesus. That is to say, I am obliged to try and state a clear position on the whole vexed question of historicity and mythology. My position is that the things concerning Jesus have a strong claim to be treated as weighty data for our understanding of man and the world because at their heart and as their foundation there lies the creative impact of the actual historical Jesus. I reject the notion that the things concerning Jesus are through and through nothing but ideas which men formed to constitute a cluster of interpretations more or less loosely connected with, or occasioned by, the historical figure designated by the name-phrase 'Jesus of Nazareth'.

The most reasonable and likely conclusion, I believe, is that the impact of Jesus portrayed in the New Testament and the interpretation of Jesus put forward in the New Testament arose because, by and large, Jesus was the sort of man who actually lived the sort of life and died the sort of death which, under the conditions of Palestine in his time, would validly give rise to the impact portrayed, and the interpretations put forth, by the New Testament writers. That is to say I hold that the most valid and probable historical judgement about the New Testament is that the major constitutive event or events in its creation was, as a matter of fact, the creative living, teaching and dying of Jesus of Nazareth, and that the historical reality of the personality of Jesus is validly and effectively reflected in the New Testament writings.

My grounds for this judgement are fourfold. Firstly, when I reflect on such works of New Testament scholarship as come my way, and reflect also on my actual experience of men and communities, I do not find the thesis of the community as the primary creative force in the construction of the things concerning Jesus by any means the most credible hypothesis. It seems to me much more credible and rational to postulate an actual historical Jesus commensurate with the interpretations and responses of the community as the prior given and creative cause of the community understanding and faith. I judge that the records as they stand require an historical creative personality before they will permit of a creative responsive community.

I am, secondly, emboldened in this judgement by reflecting on the nature of the presuppositions involved in the vast mass of modern

New Testament study concerning historicity, what can be judged to have happened in history and what can be counted as plausibly historical. All these assumptions are those of the current modern mythology about the nature of the world, of reality and of human understanding. If there is a case at all for supposing, or even trying out the hypothesis, that the things concerning Jesus can constitute evidence for shaping our view of the world and man, then we are not required to succumb before we start our investigation to the presuppositions of any world-view. I am, at least, entitled to point out that in our judgements about what is or can be historical and therefore in our judgements about the most credible explanation of the New Testament evidence about Jesus we are already bringing our presuppositions to bear. When, therefore, one is engaged in questioning presuppositions, one is entitled to claim that full weight should be given to the *prima facie* evidence for the creative historical personality of Jesus *before* one starts to trim that evidence to what it is alleged is required by the modern understanding of what is historically possible or plausible.

Thirdly, I think it necessary to take account of the attitude of those who presented the evidence in the first place. It seems to me that whatever may be the form of the mythology, if it be such, in which they clothed and expressed their understanding of what they had set out, it is clear that the whole self-understanding of their faith and impact of their message turned on the fact that this 'mythology' was, so to speak, pinned to reality by the historic givenness and happenedness of Jesus (cf., e.g., the 'the Word was made flesh' of John and the 'if Christ be not risen' of Paul). They may have been quite wrong, but there can be little doubt about what they thought they were doing and about what they intended to do. Thus I find that not only does the evidence of the New Testament as a whole most reasonably require the historical impact of the creative personality of Jesus, but that those who bear witness to this have this as their necessary presupposition.

Fourthly, and finally, I am personally the more ready to accept the witness of the New Testament writers to the historically based nature of their understanding of Jesus because I find in practice that their writings serve to re-create in me and in relation to my own living, experiences, insights and occasions of a strengthening and life-enhancing nature which I can recognize as being analogous to, or continuous with, or even part of, experiences and insights to which they refer. Thus I have experiential grounds for holding them to be trustworthy witnesses to that of which they purport to speak.

But now I have moved fully into the realm of faith! None the less it is a faith with reasons, and I see no reason to count my own experiences as *less* valid than those of others. Further, the majority of my reasons for my position on historicity do not depend on this faith. And finally, I have, at this stage, only to give reasons which are sufficient for adopting a certain basis for a piece of experimental thinking. This basis is that the things concerning Jesus can reasonably be taken to be based on the historical creative personality of Jesus of Nazareth. So we are now ready to proceed in the next two lectures to consider the understanding of the world, God and man which was worked out in the first five Christian centuries on the basis of the things concerning Jesus. As we do so, we can reasonably entertain the belief that this is a constructive and creative understanding of the realities of the world and of man's situation in the world, built up from the realities of Jesus' life in the world and the realities of the life-experience and understanding of the early Christians. We are not, therefore, to consider what are simply theories or ideas of the world. We are to consider interpretations which have a claim to be taken seriously in *their* claim that they are based on given historical and experiential evidence. Alongside our glimpse of the possible universal significance of our concern for persons we are to set the claimed universal significance of Jesus. The main purpose of the argument of this lecture has been to show that there is a case for holding that the claimed universal significance of Jesus is as much based on the realities experienced in human life in the world as is the claim for the universal significance of persons.

III

The Universal Significance of Jesus

WE COME NOW to considering the understanding of the world, God
and man which was worked out in the first five centuries on the basis
of the things concerning Jesus. The chief ground for turning our
attention to this is that this understanding has, or was believed to
have, a basis in facts. That is to say that the Christian understanding
of God, man and the world is held to follow from the things concerning Jesus, while the things concerning Jesus are held to be based in the
actual serial realities of the living and dying of the historical character
known as Jesus of Nazareth. We are to examine what purports to
be the effects of the impact of the historical creative personality of
Jesus of Nazareth on some men's understanding of themselves and
of their place in the universe.

But how was it possible for the impact of one historical personality to
be decisive for a man's understanding of himself and of the world?
And if and when this is made clear can it conceivably remain a plausible
or persuasive possibility for us? This is what we have to investigate.

The impact of Jesus was understood as of universal significance
in the first place because it occurred in a particular context, namely
that of what we now call first-century Palestinian Judaism. This
context provided the set of ideas about the world and the pattern of
understanding life which made it possible to claim that Jesus was of
universal significance. I am not, at this stage, concerned with the
validity of this set of ideas and of this pattern of life-understanding,
but with their *existence*. Further, I am not suggesting, because it
would not be true to do so, that there is a precise and clear
pattern that can be designated 'first-century Palestinian Judaic

thought'. Even on the evidence we have, which is by no means complete, it is clear that the 'pattern' is one of great complexity and diversity—so much so that even to speak of 'the pattern' at all is to over-systematize and over-simplify. None the less, we may speak of the whole set of ideas current in first-century Palestine as the matrix which provided the concepts which made possible the identification of the universal significance of Jesus of Nazareth, or at least provided the possibility of claiming universal significance for Jesus.

Now in this whole matrix, the concept of the Messiah is clearly of fundamental importance. The first form which the claim for the universal or potentially universal significance of Jesus took was that Jesus was the Messiah, that Jesus is the Christ. For this claim to be made, two things are necessary. Firstly, that the notion of Messiah should already have a content, and secondly, that there should be things about Jesus which lead to relating that concept to his person. The notion of Messiah obtains its content from the set of thought-forms and life-understanding in which—in its turn—it has developed. And *this* context is the experience and faith of the Jewish people stretching back into the history of Israel and Judah. What the Jewish people made of this experience and history of theirs is reflected in the pages of what we now call the Old Testament.

We do not need to discuss the surely insoluble question of how much in the Old Testament is 'historical', in the sense of trying to decide, or needing to decide, whether any particular account, say of an Exodus journey, or of the reign of a particular king of Israel, provides you with data enabling you to make judgements of the 'what-you-would-have-seen-if-you-had-been-there' sort. For the purposes of my thesis we can put on one side this question about the particular historicity of particular happenings. For the essential point about the Old Testament attitude to history which is central to the content of the notion of the Messiah is this. The Old Testament portrays and reflects the development of the faith that as a matter of fact God controls history for the sake of his people. This, of course, is one of the ideas which is widely held at the present time to be an unthinkable one. It is necessary, therefore, to reiterate that I am not at present discussing validity or even 'thinkability' but simply existence as a fact in the history of ideas. I shall hope, in due course, to display my grounds for taking this idea seriously now. Meanwhile, there is no need to go into details about particular instances of the historical weightiness of the Old Testament. The fundamental point is that the Old Testament makes it clear that the Jewish view of the world which was still flourishing in the Palestine of Jesus of Nazareth had built into it the belief that the facts, events, happenings of history were susceptible of, and conformable to, a personal purpose. This purpose was personal in a twofold sense. Firstly, the serial happenings which constituted the history of the Jewish people were held to be moving, or to be capable of being moved, in a direction which fulfilled the life of the Jewish people (and perhaps the life of all men). Secondly, there was held to be a mover of the events of history towards this personal end (sc. end involving persons) who could be thought of as personal, in the sense that this mover was concerned with this personal end and to this end was concerned to enter into a reciprocal relationship with the persons involved in the end.

The concept which most conveniently focuses the Jewish understanding of the world through this understanding of the personal purposes related to history is that of the Kingdom of God. This concept is most convenient for our purposes because there can be no reasonable historical doubt that the idea of the Kingdom of God played a central part both in the thinking of Jesus and in the initial thinking about Jesus. The Kingdom of God stands for that realm in which there is finally achieved and established those purposes of God for his people which were discovered in their history and which it was believed would be worked out through their history. The Kingdom of God was the situation in which, or the state of affairs through which, God would establish everything in full accordance with the pattern of personal purpose which stemmed from his own being. This pattern was something which the Jews believed they had learnt from their experiences of their history in and through which God had made himself and his purposes known to them. To achieve this understanding and knowledge of God, they had needed the insight and discernment of inspired men, but this prophetic insight, they believed, had led to the perception of the real pattern of God's activity which was the expression of the reality of God's being. Prophetic insight had given true perception which led to real knowledge about God because that prophetic insight was itself God-given. Since it was the true pattern of the real expression of God's being which was perceived in and through their history the Jews were quite clear that this pattern would be fulfilled in the final pattern which history produced, and that they would have a real share in this pattern. It was this final pattern which was thought of and expected under the notion of the establishment by God of his Kingdom. The true pattern of the being and activity of the living God has been experienced and discovered by the Jews in and through their history. Therefore this pattern was bound to be established. God had been truly met with in history, therefore history was bound eventually, to produce God's purpose. God would establish his Kingdom.

What is important here is the structure and the internal logic of the thought and of the whole approach to the world and of the understanding of life involved in this way of thinking. The *truth* of this way of understanding the world and the life of the world is clearly not finally or decisively verifiable. The very structure of the thinking itself precludes this. For the truth of this understanding of the world is not finally and fully established until there is produced out of history that state of affairs in which everything is fully in accordance with the pattern of the being of God. But that state of affairs is the final establishment of the Kingdom of God, and the establishment of the Kingdom of God is what is confidently looked for. Therefore it is clear that this faith of the Jews that God controls history for the sake of his people, i.e. that history reflects, and is, or can be, related to, a personal purpose, is not a truth *statement*. It is not something which is based, or can be based, adequately on a demonstrable existing and observable state of affairs. But although this faith about a God active in history does not involve a truth *statement*, it is exceedingly important to notice that it does involve a truth *claim*. The Jewish faith in any form which is continuous with the internal logical structure developed in, and reflected in, the Old Testament is not to be understood as just an attitude to the world. It is an attitude to the world which has, as an integral feature of its structure, the claim that it is an attitude validly based on, and corresponding to, that reality which is both perceivable in the historical realities of this world, and also the reality which extends beyond, and ultimately determines, the realities of this world. The God whom the Jew faithfully knows and whose activity the Jew faithfully perceives is the true and living God, and therefore his Kingdom *will* come.

This truth claim which is tied into history because it is read out of history is so truly a truth claim that it led to the Jews finding their own history an acute problem. For this history showed no signs of verifying the truth of that which it was believed had been perceived in and through history. Hence the urgency in many Jewish circles of various forms of the hope of the appearance of the Messiah, of the coming of him who was appointed and anointed by God at least to initiate the coming of the Kingdom of God. Something *must* occur in the history of the Jewish people to make it clear that the God known in and through their history was the true God, i.e. truly there as God, and that the personal pattern discerned as at work in history would have its fulfilment. So acute was this problem of history, that round about what we now call the first centuries B.C. and A.D. many Jews were tending to submerge their distinctive understanding of history as at least potential material for the purposes of a God concerned with persons in syncretistic versions of the various non-biblical faiths and philosophies current at that time. The view which these faiths and philosophies took of the world and of man is something which we shall have to consider in relation to the development of the Christian understanding of these matters. At this stage it is sufficient to note that the distinctive biblical understanding of history as the sphere of the activity of a God concerned with persons and as the source of material which could be productive of personal purposes and patterns was under very great threat. What evidence was there to sustain this faith in the living God actively involved in events against the actual course of events in Judaea with its minute significance in the midst of the vastness of the Roman Empire?

Christianity arose because a small group of persons conditioned by the biblical tradition and faith which I have been describing believed that they had discovered a decisive piece of evidence, to wit that God had sent his Messiah and that the Messiah was Jesus. The basis of the discovery of the universal significance of Jesus of Nazareth lay in the identification of him as the Lord's Messiah, as the Christ of God. This had universal significance because of the understanding of the world, history and man which lay behind the Messianic expectations of the Jews. And these Messianic expectations arose because the Jews believed that they had been led to discover through their history the true pattern of the being and activity of the true God. Without this context, background and tradition no claim to the universal significance of Jesus of Nazareth could have arisen. But the claim that the Messiah *has* come because Jesus is the Messiah does not only presuppose this pattern of thought, understanding and faith. The claim that Jesus is the Messiah is also a claim that this pattern of thought, understanding and faith is valid. God is rightly and not mistakenly known as active in history for the fulfilment of a personal and purposive pattern.

Once again, therefore, we have a truth claim and not just the assertion of a particular attitude couched in a particular mythology. Moreover, we have here a truth claim which is based on what is clearly held to be a truth statement, viz. that Jesus is, as a matter of fact, the Messiah. For the discovery that this Jesus of Nazareth is the Christ is clearly understood as the recognition of a fact. It was a fact which came to be recognized as such by the cumulative effect of other observations. Jesus' conduct of his own life made it clear that he believed himself to have a mission in connection with the coming of the Kingdom of God. His teaching and actions were concerned with the nature of that Kingdom and that coming, with the presence of the power of that Kingdom, and with the response required to the coming of the Kingdom. His actions in challenging the established authorities and in following that challenge up by what became his last journey to Jerusalem, and the interpretation which he put upon the fate which threatened him during his meal with his disciples before his arrest, makes it sufficiently historically clear that he came to see his death as part of the pattern of his mission in connection with the coming of the Kingdom of God.

Thus we can have little doubt that in his self-understanding Jesus saw both his living and his dying as centrally associated with

God's bringing in of his Kingdom. So many people have found this whole complex of ideas either unthinkable or else thinkable only when it has been translated into a demythologized version which represents the modern guess at the currently acceptable categories which can most plausibly be alleged to *be* a translation of the original, that it has been claimed that the evidence for the fact that Jesus did think in this way is of the shakiest. But this is the result of a grave confusion of thought which does more credit to a misdirected respect for Jesus on the part of those who think this way, than to their powers of historical judgement. In fact, the evidence that Jesus did so understand and direct his life is quite satisfactorily strong. The difficulty is that so much turns on whether his understanding and living was justified, authentic and valid or not. Many people find it impossible to believe that the sort of question posed by the living and dying of Jesus, understood in the way in which it seems very probable that he himself understood it, can be posed at all. They therefore hold that it cannot historically be the case that he lived in such a way or understood his living in such a way. But this is simply to allow sufficiently probabilified historical data to succumb to current prejudice. '*I* cannot think like that, therefore Jesus cannot have thought like that whatever the evidence may suggest'. Such an attitude directed, say, to Napoleon or Augustus Caesar, would be immediately laughed out of court. But then one's judgement of the historical nature of the existence of Napoleon or Augustus Caesar does not necessarily affect one's judgement about the nature of historical existence as such. The difficulty clearly lies in the implications of the tradition which is the context of the life of Jesus and with which Jesus identified himself. The difficulty lies not in the shakiness of the evidence but in what the evidence might be evidence for. For what is at issue is whether there is evidence that there is a God who is active in history for the fulfilment of a personal and purposive pattern.

Jesus was recognized as such evidence because of the pattern of his living and dying seen in the context of the biblical and Jewish understanding of the world. This tradition provided a context which made the identification of Jesus or someone else as the Messiah a possibility. But it was the actual pattern of Jesus' living and dying which gave to the notion of Messiah both content and existential actuality. The recognition of Jesus as the Messiah was the recognition of a fact and the recognition of this fact anchored the biblical and Jewish interpretation of history in the sheer serial givenness of history.

But we still have to reckon with the fact that the recognition of Jesus as the Messiah did not simply arise out of the pattern of his living and dying, up to his death on a cross. The pattern of his living and dying had to place him in a Kingdom of God context and therefore within the scope of the notion of Messiahship before any recognition of him as Messiah could occur. But the relevant records indicate that Jesus was first decisively, rather than tentatively, recognized as the Messiah when a comparative handful of people among those who had been associated with him became convinced that the cross on which he had died had not terminated the pattern and the purpose of Jesus' life. Their conviction, based on evidence which they seemed to some extent to be able to share and to discuss and recognize in common, was that 'God had raised him up'. They believed they had evidence that the understanding, commitment and direction of the life of Jesus had not terminated in his death on the cross, but was continued in his livingness, known to his immediate followers and to be made known as widely as possible in the world at large.

Here again it is important to notice that this discovery of the resurrection of Jesus was taken to be the discovery of a fact. This is made sufficiently clear by the famous, or perhaps it should nowadays be the notorious, story of the empty tomb. If this story in its various versions is at all historically accurate then it reflects one of the series of events and experiences through which the discouraged followers of Jesus became persuaded that he was in fact not dead and finished, but alive and purposefully active. If this does not recount one of the events which caused belief in the Resurrection, but rather reflects the Resurrection belief in story form, then it still reflects the fact that this belief in its initial form, however it was caused, did include the claim that the Resurrection, whatever else it might be, was a fact in a series of events. Thus it is sufficiently clear, although to us no doubt unpleasingly clear, that the recognition of Jesus as the Messiah was held to be the discovery of a fact. This discovery arose out of the cumulative effect of a whole set of things concerning Jesus. These included the pattern and direction of his living and dying, together with the self-understanding displayed by Jesus and the set of experiences common within a strictly limited class of followers which added up to the recognition of the fact of the Resurrection. Thus it was proclaimed as a fact that God has raised up Jesus and so made it decisively clear that Jesus was the Messiah. This fact about Jesus was thus held to be the decisive fact in the whole world. It constituted *the* good news, that is to say the Gospel.

As I have shown, the possibility of such a truth claim being made which was at the same time a claim to universal significance could only have arisen within a tradition which had evolved such an understanding of God, the world and man as was to be found in the Judaism which expected the coming of the Kingdom of God. This was a way of looking at the world which implied the belief that it is history which produces the key to the cosmos, for history provides material in and through which the Lord God works out the pattern of his personal purposes. It was a belief which had grown up out of history and through history and had led the Jews to look *to* history. What some men in this Jewish tradition discovered was that the facts concerning the man Jesus of Nazareth led to the recognition of this man as God's Messiah, that is to say, the person in history who has the rôle of bringing God's purpose in history to its climax.

Now if we try to take a glance at the whole gamut of events which might properly be held to fall within the scope of human history, we must surely be inclined to conclude that the very notion of 'history as a whole' is an empty one and that the suggestion that history provides the material for the working out of the pattern of a personal purpose is absurd. To suggest further that one historical personage is both the vindication of the existence of this personal purpose and the definition of the nature of that purpose, is simply to put forward the absurdity of absurdities. Theoretically, that is to say looked at apart from particular facts, there would seem to be very much to be said for this view. But there are some particular facts which count obstinately against the absurdity and for the truth of this view. Firstly, there is the evolution of the Jewish understanding of the world and history through the Jews' experience of their history. Secondly, there is the pattern of the living and dying of Jesus placed within and orientated towards that understanding of the world and history. And thirdly, there is the discovery that Jesus' understanding and mission was vindicated by the fact that his dying had been superseded by his living.

But, we may feel obliged to say, the Resurrection cannot be true, cannot be a fact and cannot be discovered. *That* precisely is the question. Some people held that it was true because it was discovered to be a fact or discovered itself as a fact. Before we are quite sure that this *must* be absurd we should consider that many people today are ready to accept the Sartreian absurdity that all life and all reality is absurd. Why should the Sartreian absurdity of meaninglessness be more reasonably acceptable than the Christian absurdity of meaningfulness, especially when we consider the weight of that area of reality to which our concern for persons directs us, especially too, when the Christian gospel does not either proceed from absurdity or point to absurdity? The Christian gospel proceeds from what can reasonably be claimed to be data thrown up within a particular historical series and focused within a particular historical life. And the Christian gospel points to an understanding of God, the world, and man which can be seen to be consistent with that openness, perseverance and hope which I have already referred to as a recognizable option in our assessment of the human situation.

I shall try to portray this direction of the Christian Gospel in some faint measure in my last two lectures. I shall argue in more detail about the conflict between meaningfulness and absurdity in my fifth and sixth lectures. I am at the moment engaged in arguing the case for giving a hearing to the claim for the universal significance of Jesus discovered to be the Christ of God and for not dismissing *a priori* the possibility of the discovery of his Resurrection. I want now to continue to investigate the weight of this claim concerning the resurrected Jesus Christ by outlining its creative effect in the understanding of God, the world and man in the centuries immediately following its first appearance. I am quite clear that we can never finally know, at any rate in this world, that Jesus is the Christ. We have no final truth statement, only a truth claim. We are, of course, investigating the Christian *faith*. But a truth claim is the more authenticated the more it can be shown to have a creative and life-enhancing effect on and through those who entertain it and assert it.

Thus we turn to consider the creative effect of accepting it as true that Jesus is the Christ.

The recognition that Jesus is the Christ means that one discovers not only that Jesus is the Christ but also that there is a Christ and he is Jesus. Thus this recognition not only establishes the actual and historical existence of the Messiah, but also defines the nature and content of this existence. We have an ostensive definition of Messiahship which at the same time reinforces and establishes the historical relevance and involvement of the whole way of looking at the world which had produced the historical expectation of the historical appearance of the Messiah. So the discovery that this particular Jesus of Nazareth is the Messiah reinforces that understanding of the world which sees history as providing the material for the working out of the pattern of the purposes of a personal God. Hence there is a working vindication of the belief that history produces the key to the cosmos and an essential reinforcement of the faith that *this* attitude to the world is a truthful response to the way things really are, to the ultimate and decisive nature of reality. But, further, as there is an actually lived out pattern of the life of Jesus, we have in his historical personality the pattern of the key to the cosmos. To discover that this Jesus is the Christ is to discover the fact that is determinative of one's understanding of all other facts. (It is *not* a fact which allows us to deny or ignore other facts; the escapism in the face of facts which Christians in practice tend to share with other human beings is to be discussed later.)

This determining nature of the existence of Jesus for the understanding of, and approach to, all existence is the central implication of the recognition of Jesus as the Christ, but it was an implication which had to be realized, sustained and then creatively maintained over against, and in fruitful relationship with, the current world-understandings of the world in which Christianity came to life.

The structure of the development of this implication of the discovered fact that Jesus is the Christ can be seen in the sequence of affirmations about Jesus which gradually became systematized in the course of the first five centuries. Alongside the discovery that Jesus is the Christ there arises the affirmation that Jesus is Lord. The term 'Lord' used in this context has, naturally, a complex history of its own. But this we need not study, for it is sufficiently clear that the statement 'Jesus is Lord' is logically a translation of 'Messiah' into a term which has the possibility of a much wider understanding than the Jewish term, even in its Greek form Christ. Thus 'Jesus is Lord' means that Jesus is the determining fact concerning the proper understanding of existence in the world and in history.

But this proper understanding includes the reinforcement of the discovery that history produces the key to the cosmos. Hence the affirmation 'Jesus is Lord' demands that the Christian understanding of the cosmos shall both fight with, and come to terms with, all other understandings of the cosmos. In the first five centuries this dialogue which is also a battle, and conflict which is also a creative construction, focuses on the further affirmation that Jesus is the Logos. Jesus is the key to the understanding of the cosmos, of the realm of things, as well as to the understanding of history, the realm of persons, *and the understanding of these two realms must be united*. It is here that the real battle was fought in the fourth and fifth centuries and it is here, as I hope to show in the second half of the lectures, that the real battle is still being fought.

How are we to understand our human situation? Is it the realm of things, the proper subject matter of a deterministic science, which finally defines reality? Or is it the realm of persons with possibilities, even in history, of openness, perserverance and hope? Or must we conclude that, for the sake of personalness, we have to have one approach to the realm of things and another to the realm of persons and that there can be no constructive reconciliation between them? That is to say, must we affirm personalness in the face of the fact that reality as a whole is ultimately absurd? It is to the fourth and fifth century version of this debate that I shall devote my next lecture. The debate took the form of a debate about the status of Jesus. But, as I shall show, this debate was not at all a series of metaphysical mystifications. It was a debate which was about what are our questions too. For on the basis of the things concerning Jesus, Christianity opposes the view that it is nature and not history, the realm of things and not the realm of persons, which ultimately determines reality. Christianity also opposes the view that, in the end, reality is absurd.

IV

God, Man and the World – and the God-Man

TO DISCOVER THAT Jesus is the Christ is to discover the fact that is determinative of one's understanding of all other facts. This is the universal significance of Jesus which follows from the events of his living, dying and Resurrection. For these events identify Jesus as the historical personality upon whom and through whom there is focused the personal purposes of the God who is active to bring out of the stuff of history the pattern of personal fulfilment. Thus, if Jesus is the Christ, then Jesus is Lord, the personal existence who is significant not only for Jews who expect a Messiah to vindicate the meaning of history, but also for Gentiles, whatever expectation or lack of it their particular world-views encourage. For as the Christ has appeared as an actual historical existence, the belief that history produces the key to the meaning of existence in the world has been vindicated. So the factual and historical existence of Jesus Christ claims a determining significance for all men's understanding of the cosmos. This is the meaning asserted for the existence of Jesus Christ because it is the meaning implied by the existence of Jesus Christ. We have now to consider how this meaning of the givenness of Jesus Christ made its way and unfolded its further implications in engagement with men's understandings of their existence in the world of the Graeco-Roman civilization of the second to fifth centuries.

Both Jews and Greeks had evolved a belief that man in his peculiar humanness and the universe in its peculiar givenness either did essentially fit together or were ultimately capable of being fitted together. To have a belief that man and the universe fit together is to imply a presupposed understanding that it sometimes makes sense to set men and the universe over against one another. Seeing that 'the universe' ought to mean 'everything there is' and men must be included in 'everything there is', it seems odd that it should ever make sense to set 'men' and 'the universe' over against one another. But this is really to try to use a logical quibble to step aside from an existential problem. It is clear enough that men have found and do find the world a problem. That is to say they find that their existence in the world is a problem to themselves. The universe, in the sense of everything there is, is constantly posing problems to men in their humanness. Men find that the things which matter to them are swept aside, disturbed, frustrated by 'things in general'. We are here back to the problems which I discussed in my first lecture, when I referred to those things in our understanding of the world and of the life in the world which count against, or work against, our awareness of the supreme importance of the things concerning personalness. We are back also to the question of the Absurd which is indeed the same question. Man finds his existence in the world a problem to him. Is there an answer to this problem? Do men and the universe fit together? In our discussion of this during the second half of the lectures, we shall be considering mainly the way Western thought has developed on this problem, but we shall clearly have to consider also what may be called the Oriental suggestion that the problem is to be solved by learning how to transcend and ignore it. The solution lies in losing the problem by realizing that the problem is an illusion created by the illusion of desire for an answer. At present, however, we must confine our attention to the historical development of Christian thinking in its early setting.

Christianity, then, made its way in a world which was heir to two major ways of thinking about how men and the universe fitted together. The Jews believed that the tie-up occurred in and through history, because history provided the material out of which God produced the pattern of his purpose which was concerned with the fulfilment of persons. Men and universe fitted together because God so fitted them. God is thought of as the Creator who is responsible for the beginning of the universe, the Judge who is responsible for the end, and the Saviour who can be relied upon to take such action as will ensure the achievement of his personal purposes. An expression of this understanding of things is to be found in the looking for the Kingdom of God and the hope of the coming of the Messiah which we have discussed at length in the previous lecture. The tie-up between things as they are and what men require for their fulfilment occurs through history because God can be relied upon to bring about this tie-up.

The main answer to this problem in the tradition of Greek thinking was rather different. The tie-up between man and the universe did not occur through the activity of God, it was a fact because of the existence of rationality. The faith here was not a developing faith in God but a pre-supposed faith in reason. The universe *was* a universe, a whole which could be thought about coherently and *as* a whole because it was ordered. It had, basically, harmony and pattern, and therefore unity. It was, in fact, the *cosmos*, the ordered and comprehensible whole. Now that which on the one hand produces an ordered and patterned whole and on the other hand appreciates order and pattern, is reason, which is precisely concerned with order, measurement and pattern.

There was one common word for reason, both in the sense of that basic ordering of the universe which made understanding possible, and in the sense of the human capacity to arrange matters in order and so to understand. The same word, too, was used of the speech which both formulates and conveys meaning. This word was *logos*. Man and the universe fitted together because of the *logos* of the *cosmos*. The universe had an underlying essential and rational unity. Man had an essential affinity with this ordering rationality of the universe by virtue of his reason, which was what distinguished him from every other existing thing. And by the ordered and ordering exercise of his reason, man could lay bare his essential affinity with the universe and live in harmony with it and in it. This understanding of the way man and the universe fitted together took on various forms, from the immanentism of the Stoics to the transcendentalism of the Platonists, but we have time to consider only the basic structure of the understanding. The Jew, whether or not he had come to give reason a part to play in his understanding of the world, put his faith in God. The Greek, whether or not he believed in God, put his faith in reason.

At the time when Jesus of Nazareth was born and in the subsequent years, the Jewish faith worked up to an acute historical crisis with the final capture of Jerusalem by the Romans in A.D. 70 and the final abortive revolt of the second century. Among some, the Jewish faith in God survived triumphantly, but the hope of history and the hope in history lay quiescent as far as the general history of Western thought about the world went until we come to such a secularized form as Marxism. (Here is a line of inquiry which we cannot now pursue.) Others among the Jews became so disillusioned in their whole faith through the actual course of historical events, that they abandoned all belief in the God of their fathers as a God who in any sense tied together the affairs and events of this world and the true concerns of men. Such Jews shared in, and contributed to, the growth of a very widespread and variegated religious development which is characteristic of the climate of thought in which Christianity developed, and which is known generally as Gnosticism.

The sources of the particular forms of Gnosticism are as various as are the many religions and philosophical systems which were to be found flourishing in the Roman and Hellenistic civilizations which existed round the Mediterranean and stretched as far East as the Indus. But we are concerned only with the basic structure of the common answer which all these forms gave to the problem of man and the world. This answer took the shape which it did, and gained the currency which it did, because of the collapse of the Greek faith (if I may be allowed so to call it for ease of reference) in reason, which was, of course, far more widespread and general than the Jewish faith in God. We shall, therefore, now confine our attention to the development of the Christian understanding of the things concerning Jesus in relation to the problems posed by the world-understandings current in Graeco-Roman thought, and shall no longer be concerned with the development in Judaism. In thus turning aside from Judaism, we shall not only be following the course of historical development, we shall also be following out the logic of the discovery that Jesus is the Christ. For if Jesus is the Christ, then the future of the living understanding of the way in which God uses history as material for the production of the pattern of his personal purposes lies in its main stream with the things concerning Jesus, and not with Judaism which has failed to identify the fact of facts, viz., that the Messiah *is* Jesus.

I refer to this turning aside from Judaism in this rather pointed way so that it may be quite clear that the logic of the things concerning Jesus does involve what many people hold to be the scandalously offensive claim that these things hold a decisive key to the proper understanding of man's existence in the universe. Nothing is to be gained by concealing this scandalous fact, for it arises from the very particularity, concreteness and historicity of the basis of the things concerning Jesus. *This* data and no other is finally decisive for our true understanding of man and the world. Since it is the thesis of these lectures that it is here that the very strength of Christianity lies, I can scarcely be expected to conceal it, even if the claim involves a scandal which constitutes a particular obstacle to the acceptance of the claim. I would just ask once again for suspension of judgement and openness of mind. Let us follow the way the claim works before we reject it *a priori*. Further, I hope to show in the last two lectures how the exclusiveness of the claim of Christianity is to be related to a way of life whose aim is total openness.

Christianity, therefore, as heir to the Jewish hope of history and in history, enters upon a world in which there is less and less belief that man and the universe fit together. In the complexity and vastness of the Roman Empire, men had found it more and more difficult to believe that the underlying pattern of things was reasonable or that men could, by the use of their reason alone, penetrate to any unchanging pattern of existence beyond the complexity and perplexity of the change and decay in the midst of which they lived. The very orderliness and unchangingness of the heavens which had once seemed evidence of the celestial harmony of the cosmos to be enjoyed by reason had somehow taken on the aspect of a relentless and implacable fate which maintained all the processes and events of the universe in a fixed order which had no concern with or place for personal development and fulfilment. Moreover, society had become too mixed, changing and large for men to find themselves at home in a manner which could give them any confidence that things in general had any room for their particular personal concerns. The various philosophical ways which had once been thought of as ways to answering the problem of existence in the discovery of abiding truth were still followed, but generally without much serenity or assurance. For many, especially in the big cities, such ways were in any case above them, so they turned to any cult which had a sufficient veneer of philosophy to look like an answer, or to any mythology of one tradition or another which looked religiously authoritative. Here men sought to find a revealed answer to the problem of their existence which would lift them out of their homelessness in an alien universe, and give them the opportunity to come to terms with the conditions of their own existence, in a way productive of peaceful and hopeful living. Everywhere and at every level of sophistication and credulity there was a search for Gnosis, for the knowledge which would tell a man where he came from, what was his true end, and how, in the midst of the existence thrust upon him, he could find his way to the true end by escaping from the alienation of his actual existence to the fulfilment of his essential being.

By virtue of their common feature of claiming to offer this saving knowledge (*gnosis*), the vast range of philosophies, theosophies, cults and magical systems which developed at this time are given the generic name of Gnosticism. They had, as I have already suggested, a basic structure to the answer which they gave to the problem of man and the world. Both the world and history were to be despaired of. Reality is essentially dualistic. The true spiritual reality of man has somehow got mixed up with, and trapped in, a world of matter and a series of events to which his essential self is wholly alien. If there is any hope for man at all it must lie in a complete escape from the alien matter of history and the indifferent, or more likely positively malignant, matter of the cosmos. It is because of this dualistic despair of both the universe and history that Gnosticism constitutes the meeting point of the Jew disillusioned with history, the Greek disillusioned with reason, and the Oriental who never believed that man and the cosmos fitted together in any case.

But Christianity had arisen with the discovery that Jesus was the Christ and therefore was committed to a reinvigorated and re-defined view of history as the sphere of the working out of a personal purpose and, as such, productive of the key to the cosmos. Hence the discovery made in and through a Jewish context that Jesus was the Christ had to be translated into the more widely comprehensible claim that Jesus Christ was Lord, definitive of any man's understanding of history and the cosmos.

In maintaining and developing their understanding of Jesus Christ as Lord within the sort of context which I have been very briefly describing in my discussion of Gnosticism, Christians of the second century found themselves picking up a Greek notion which was still viable, although it was no longer an unchallenged axiom of thought. This notion was that men and the universe fit together because of the Logos of the cosmos. Men had sought through many philosophical channels to become clear about and to respond to the Logos. But it was Christians who had found him, or rather, been found by him. Jesus Christ is the Logos of the cosmos.

To make such an assertion two things are required. Firstly, there must be the discovery that Jesus Christ is given as definitive of our understanding of the world and of our place and hope in it. I have sketched out the structure of the way in which this discovery arose. Secondly, there must be in existence a way of looking at the world and of understanding man's place in the world which gives content to the notion of 'the Logos of the cosmos'. I have *very* briefly sketched out the structure of the background to this notion. Now this second notion clearly reflects what men at some period found thinkable. Indeed it actually sums up the structure of their thinking. It was a very widely taken-for-granted notion and authoritative as such. Thus it represents one of the then currently respectable cosmic intuitions or cosmic myths. Men assumed that the universe was in some sense rational, i.e. tied up with the distinctive humanness of human beings. Or else they believed that it was, or hoped that it was, or feared that it was not. For, as I have already indicated, this way of looking at the world was, in the first centuries of our era, under heavy threat, or actually abandoned by many. None the less, it made sense to search for the Logos of the cosmos. It represented a comprehensible, a thinkable view of the world which could, therefore, be asserted or denied in a meaningful way.

The second and third century development of the Logos doctrine in connection with the things concerning Jesus is typical of the pragmatic manner in which Christian thought develops. This development might be called accidental. I would maintain that it should properly be called experimental, proceeding by means of the various groups of data available and thereby finding out what the data is good for. In the definitive witness to the things concerning Jesus which had crystallized out into what we call the New Testament, the *term* 'Logos' had been used by the writer of the Fourth Gospel to express his insight that Jesus was definitive of both history and cosmos because of his role in relation to the Old Testament understanding of God and the world. He prefaces his gospel with an introduction which makes use of this term (whose English translation is usually given as *Word*) in such a way as to make it clear that he is aware that the term 'Word' both fits into biblical and Jewish talk about God, the world and history, and has the chance of fitting into Greek talk about the world and rationality. In prefacing his exposition of the things concerning Jesus with the sentence 'the Word became flesh' the author is making use of a creative insight into the implications of the discovery that Jesus is the Christ. It is an insight which serves as the basis for a tying together of the Jewish understanding of the world with the Greek understanding of the cosmos in a new and creative synthesis which is stimulated by and based on the things concerning Jesus.

The Christian apologists of the second and third centuries developed this insight much further for, for reasons which I have sketched, the pressing questions of their time forced them to be concerned with the cosmic significance of the things concerning Jesus. As one now studies the way in which they developed their arguments about Jesus Christ as the Logos of the cosmos, it becomes very clear that the term 'Logos' was so useful precisely because it was a very ambiguous one. The *term* appeared in the Greek version of the Old Testament, in the preface to the Fourth Gospel, and in various philosophical contexts with Platonic, Stoic and other flavours. But, of course, it operated with different meanings in the different contexts precisely because the different contexts were differing ways of looking at the world. Thus it often seems that theology proceeds by puns. For example, the Jew is desperately concerned with the Word of God (Greek: *Ho Logos tou theou*). The Stoically inclined Greek, say, is much concerned to live according to the rational shape of the cosmos (Greek: to live—*kata ton Logon*). Call Jesus Christ the Logos and you have satisfied the Jew and excited the Greek. But it really all is a matter of words, of a convenient pun.

My point is that this is not so. Rather, given that Jesus is the Christ and therefore the definitive fact for the human understanding of both history and cosmos, then the second and third century apologists had every reason for expressing this and exploring the implications of this in the language of the cosmic intuitions, of the world-understandings, of their time. But the decisive question was whether Jesus Christ would turn out to be the decisive fact for understanding the human situation in the world, or whether the current world-understandings would, in the end, place the things concerning Jesus Christ in *their* context. That is to say, would the current mythology determine the understanding of the things concerning Jesus Christ, or would the things concerning Jesus Christ be able to assert their fact-like properties sufficiently to make a decisive and definitive modification of the mythology? I have no doubt that it is the essential property of the things concerning Jesus that they do, under the inspiration of God, succeed in controlling every mythology in the interests of human openness, freedom and fulfilment. What I mean by this, it is the task of the second half of the lectures to demonstrate. Here and now I am concerned to outline the way in which the things concerning Jesus gave a new and decisive look to the current world understandings of the early centuries.

The existence and significance of Jesus Christ gave renewed grounds for the belief that men and the world fitted together. The Logos-language was a way of talking about the fitting-together of men and the world. It was, therefore, both natural and proper to use this Logos-language to express the discovered truth about Jesus. But the way in which the Logos-language was used to describe Jesus, and thus to describe his significance for the proper understanding of the world and of man's life in it, must be consistent with and, indeed, required by, the basic given shape of the things concerning

Jesus. The control for the use of the cosmic intuitions and understandings which gave the original meanings to the Logos-language
had to come from the original tradition which had made possible the
recognition of Jesus as the Messiah, which had been vindicated by
the fact that there was a Messiah because the Messiah was Jesus, and
which had been re-defined by the actual shape of the life of this
Jesus. Unless this control was maintained, there would be no given
grounds in the world and in history for our attitude to the world and
to history other than the fact that we have these attitudes. It would
simply be a question of one mythology coming to terms with another
mythology in order to produce a third which would simply last until
fashions in thinking changed once again.

Christianity, however, did not allow the Greek fashion of thinking,
which optimistically assumed the universe was rational, to be dis-
placed by the Gnostic fashion of thinking which pessimistically
assumed that men and the world did not fit together. The Gnostics
insisted on, or assumed, a complete dualism between the truly
spiritual and human on the one hand and the givenness of material
things and of the events of history on the other. The Christian on the
basis of Jesus Christ made what was essentially an optimistic assertion in a new way. He insisted that somehow the truly human and
spiritual must be understood to be related positively and hopefully to
the materiality of things and the happenings of history. One way of
doing this in the thought-forms then existing was to insist that Jesus
Christ was the Logos of the cosmos and thereby to define the Logos
of the cosmos by Jesus Christ.

But here the current ways of thinking which existed independently
of the things concerning Jesus Christ fought back, and that within
the Christian Church, to produce the acute crisis of the fourth
century which was known as Arianism. Even Greek optimism had
not conceived that man and the cosmos fitted together in a way that
took account of the material and bodily side of man, still less that
took account of the serial events of history. It was the purely
spiritual, rational, and mind side of man which was related to the
underlying spiritual and rational pattern of the universe, and which
was capable of ignoring the meaningless recurrence of the events of
history and of penetrating the mere appearance of material things

and so reaching the reality of true and absolute Being. God could never be thought of as in any way involved with the stuff of material things and the events of history, nor could value be found in or through such things. Thus, when Jesus Christ, who had been identified in his original context as the Son of God, because of his unique obedience to his unique rôle in relation to the bringing in of the Kingdom of God, was shown on the basis of this role to be also the Logos of the cosmos, a revulsion of feeling set in.

The original records about Jesus Christ made it clear that he was subject to human limitations and very much involved in the stuff both of materiality and of history. Arius and his followers who wished to retain the name of Christian (for there is something very attractive about Jesus Christ) while retaining also the assumptions of pagans (for there is something very attractive about thinking what everybody easily and currently finds thinkable) concluded that Jesus Christ could not be the true Son of God nor indeed the true Logos in the sense of the true pattern of the one, true, absolute and trans-cendent God. Rather, he could be the Son of God and the Logos of the cosmos only in the derived and watered-down sense that he had been created in a special and unique way in order to be responsible for all other creating, and capable of involvement in materiality and history.

Such a theory is pure mythology of the crudest sort which assumes that God, ultimate reality and absolute values cannot be related to the world or men, that is, to anything less than or other than himself, but that the gap can be bridged by an invented super-creature who is neither here nor there. As well as being nonsense in itself, such a mythology is straightforwardly contradictory of the Christian understanding of God and the world required by the things concerning Jesus. Jesus Christ makes it plain that history produces the key to the cosmos and that the pattern and power of the Kingdom of God is focused on a being who, however else he is to be understood, is certainly a man involved in materiality and history. Thus, however contradictory the notion of such an involvement of ultimate reality and absolute value in materiality and history might be to current ways of thinking, the things concerning Jesus demand that the notion should not only be thought, but also be asserted as true. And it was this Christian implication and assertion which Athanasius helped the Christian Church to make and to focus on the famous or notorious word *homoousios* which is translated in the Creed as 'of one substance'. Jesus Christ is 'of one substance with the Father', that is to say, he is truly Son of God and truly the Logos of the cosmos. He is truly representative of, and definitive of, the God who makes sense of history, truly representative of the pattern which fits together men and the universe. Conversely this means that whatever men have hitherto found thinkable they must now understand that God, however much he is to be thought of as the ultimately and the absolutely valuable, however much he is to be thought of as other than the events of history or the stuff of materiality, is also to be thought of as involved in, concerned with, and active through, things and happenings. Transcendence is no necessary bar to immanence, materiality is no necessary bar to spirituality, and change and process are no necessary bar to absoluteness and fulfilment. In fact, man and the universe fit together because of the involvement of God to that end.

But having reached this understanding of God and the world as required by the things concerning Jesus, the Christians were then faced with further acute problems. If Jesus Christ was rightly understood as the involvement of God in history and materiality for the sake of man, how could his person, his historical existence, be understood? This was the subject of the christological debates, the sometimes bitter discussion concerning the person of Jesus Christ, which culminated in 451 in the Definition of the Council of Chalcedon. In closing this lecture I must outline the structure of this Definition. The meaning of the Definition and the truth-claims which it makes on the basis of the things concerning Jesus are to be explored throughout the second half of the lectures.

The Definition stated that the existence who is Jesus Christ our Lord, and who is identical with the Jesus of Nazareth of the gospel records, is rightly and necessarily to be understood as truly and fully God, truly and fully man, and truly and fully one. The focusing formula of this is usually translated into English as 'one person in two natures'. Until we have had time to discuss this, both the terms 'person' and 'nature' as here used must be understood more or less as ciphers. 'Person' stands for 'one existent reality', in fact for the personal and historical individual designated Jesus of Nazareth. 'Nature' stands for all that is required to be truly God and all that is required to be truly a man. Thus the Definition asserts that the proper Christian understanding is that our Lord Jesus Christ who is Jesus of Nazareth is all that is required to be God and all that is required to be a man. It also goes on to state that all that is required to be God does not contradict, diminish or distort all that is required to be man, and all that is required to be man does not conflict with or lessen or alter all that is required to be God—and that further, the co-existence of all that is required to be God and of all that is required to be man does not mean any separation or division. There is and remains one Jesus Christ, perfect in Godhead, perfect in manhood, and perfect in unity. (One of the ways in which the Definition puts it is that 'the properties of either nature are preserved' and there is 'one and the same Lord Jesus Christ').

This is to say that to hold on to what the things concerning Jesus have shown to be true concerning the involvement of God in materiality and history for the sake of man, one must face a new and clearly articulated truth claim about the underlying structure of the relationship between God, man and the world. Briefly it is this. God is and remains all that is required to be God and this includes his absolute distinctness from everything else. God is in no sense the same thing as man or as anything that gets its existence from historicity and materiality. But in the purposes of God and by the power of God these two necessarily distinct ways of existing, of being God depending on himself and of being man depending on materiality and historicity, are drawn together into a perfection of unity which is wholly consistent with the essential requirements of each existence. We shall consider how this *could* be asserted when we explore in relation to certain trends in modern thought how something like this *can* be and *needs* to be asserted.

Meanwhile, we must rest on the first outline of the position that the structure of the definitive fact who is Jesus Christ came to be seen to be the *union* of the transcendent reality of God and the historico-material reality of man without the reduction of the one to the other. We shall have to see if this is meaningful by investigating its implications for our understanding of our human existence within the realities of the universe and of history. This investigation, I believe, will show that the things concerning Jesus which build up to the articulation of the Chalcedonian Definition lead us to understand that all theology may, as Feuerbach said, be understood as anthropology. But this is truly so only because all anthropology must be understood as theology.

V

The Exclusion of God

OUR CONCERN IS with persons. It can scarcely be otherwise. For even if we do not sufficiently know what personality is or how personalness should be defined, we are ourselves persons and cannot escape the concern which arises from being ourselves. Thus our concern is with persons even if the circumstances of our own living and the conditions of our own self-understanding lead us to treat this as a negative concern. That is to say, we may conclude that the proper policy to follow is one of detachment and withdrawal which leads to an escape from being a self and from concern with personality. But whether we consciously or unconsciously follow a policy of development of personalness or a policy of escape from personalness, as we are we cannot but be concerned with persons. The internal quality of this concern, and the external possibilities of this concern, combined with the external and internal threats to the concern, force us to see that our concern is also a question. What is it or could it be to be a person? Who am I? And what chance have I of either being myself or of escaping from myself?

Here we have what would seem to be a most subjective set of questions. Must I not decide for myself how I am to come to terms with what it is to be myself? But however unique may seem to be the self-conscious awareness of what it is to me to be myself, I have also to reckon with the fact that many aspects of me are wholly or largely continuous with that which is not me. Considered as a physical organism, I am wholly continuous with the stuff of the universe at large. *My* make-up is simply an example of the general make-up of human beings, and this is analyzable down through its various levels of organization, through cellular units, molecular units, atomic units and beyond. When one reaches this level of analysis, there is not only no difference between the units which eventually make up 'me' and those which make up 'you'; there is not even any difference between the units which make up human beings and any other organic matter. Indeed, at ultimate levels of analysis there is no difference between the units of organic and inorganic matter. In an analogous way, much, at any rate, of the physical, ethical, cultural and social features which make up the pattern which is 'I myself' is produced by, and continuous with, the larger patterns of which I am part, such as family, class, my particular society and so on. Thus I may have an intuition, which may well be supportable on a number of grounds, that I have a unique existence. It is, on the other hand, quite sufficiently clear that I have a general existence. Whatever else I may be, I am certainly simply one of the immense range of existents in the universe at large. If, therefore, I find myself facing the question 'Who am I?', I find myself facing the question of what data is available to assist me in answering the question. What is the status as data of my intuition of my uniqueness and of my caring for other persons? If I treat this sort of thing as data (and certainly it is part of the givenness of my own situation), how is it related as data to the data arrived at by forgetting my uniqueness and considering my general existence and by analyzing that into its various component parts or under its various appropriate headings? Is there, moreover, any data, anything given, which has a right to serve as definitive data, as that which is decisive for answering the question about my existence and for relating the various sorts of data to one another?

I have been arguing that the definitive data is the givenness of Jesus Christ. Or rather, I have been outlining the way in which that argument came into existence and the form which it took. I presume, certainly I hope, that in doing this I have made it clear that I am myself convinced that this is a true argument. But I hope also that I have made it clear, and shall continue to make it clear, that the argument, while it necessarily proceeds from conviction, is also an open one. This is to say, at least, that it can carry force only for those who enter into it in commitment and exploration, that it is an approach to the whole of life which cannot in this life be finally proved to be true, and that it is an argument, the direction of which is clear enough, but whose final bearing and whole fulfilment is not yet known to us. The significance of this openness of the argument for our understanding of the reality of man and of the truth of God will be considered at some length in the last two lectures. Here we are engaged in returning from our necessarily, but regrettably, brief excursion into the historical discovery and development of the force and shape of the Christian argument to our present concerns about the nature, place, scope and hope of man in the universe.

The Christian discovery on the basis of the givenness of Jesus Christ was that man and the universe hold together because of the involvement of God to that end. Thus materiality and history provide the stuff for the attainment of ultimate reality and the fulfilment of absolute value. The distinctive Christian understanding of man and the universe is that, to do justice to the realities involved therein, and to be experienced by man and through his life in the world, it is necessary to hold in distinction, and yet in union, that which is transcendent and wholly other to the universe and that which is immanent and wholly continuous with the universe. This understanding crystallized out into a doctrine of the person of Jesus Christ and has its symbol and safeguard in the fifth century Chalcedonian Definition. This is a confession of faith, an acknowledgement of what is found to be involved in responding to the givenness of Jesus Christ. Our Lord Jesus Christ is known as, and to be acknowledged as, one person in two natures. He who is the one personal existence who was historically named Jesus of Nazareth is perfect in Godhead and perfect in manhood, all that is involved in being God and all that is involved in being man. But the differences of the natures are in no way taken away by the perfection of the union and the unity. That is to say God remains God and man remains man and the absolutely fundamental difference between God in his transcendent independence and man in his dependent creatureliness is fully reaffirmed and maintained. God is God and man is man although the one Lord Jesus Christ is both—and yet one.

I shall attempt to show in the last two lectures that while this can, of course, be dismissed as unbelievable, it is by no means necessarily nonsense. I have tried in the preceding two lectures to set out the sort of grounds on which this claim came to be made. I am concerned now with the shape of what was claimed, with this twofoldness of distinction held to be in union. It is a shape of the utmost importance for our concern which I have just been recapitulating at the beginning of this lecture. It is maintained that the essential pattern of the man Jesus of Nazareth who is the Christ of God is the essential pattern of this God. The one Lord Jesus Christ exists in two natures and is all that is involved in being God and all that is involved in being man. That is to say that the name 'Jesus' not only designates the man but also designates him who is rightly thought of as being the Son of God who is 'of one substance with the Father'. The being who is Jesus Christ presents and represents the essential pattern and stuff or, if you prefer it, the true character and personality of the existence who is God. So Jesus Christ is the Logos of the cosmos. He is the presentation of that which gives the universe its shape and purpose, that indeed which ensures that it is a universe, i.e. a coherent whole. He is this because he is the embodiment and expression in materiality and history of the purpose and pattern of the God who works through materiality and history—who is Creator and Lord. Thus Jesus Christ is the expression in materiality and history of that which transcends and is independent of materiality and history. That transcendence and independence is not taken away by the involvement and identification. The properties of the Godhead are in no way diminished by the reality of the union.

On the other hand, the involvement and the union are wholly real. The properties of the manhood are in no way taken away by the union with the Godhead. Jesus is truly man, truly flesh, truly that which, biblically speaking, is created from the dust. The Bible is completely clear that man is in his physical make-up wholly continuous with the rest of the universe. Any privileged position which man enjoys or has the chance of enjoying does not proceed from his intrinsic make-up but from the possibilities which lie in his potential relationship with God. Analytically, he is a homogeneous part of the created universe. Thus Jesus Christ, because he is a man, is, like every other man, continuous as a physical organism with the whole of the rest of the universe. There is no more of an evolutionary break between the cooling of a spiral nebula and the man Jesus than there is in the case of any one of us. Between the cosmic dust and us there is no discontinuity. So Jesus Christ is all that is involved in being man including the possibility of analytical reduction to whatever are the units of the stuff of the universe.

But the Chalcedonian Definition is a symbol of the discovery and assertion that in the purposes of the transcendent and independent God, and by the power of this God, a union has been achieved between that evolutionary product of cosmic dust which is a human being and that transcendent and wholly other purposeful personalness who is God. Transcendent and independent personalness is at one with derived, dependent and evolved personality whose whole basis can be reduced to that impersonal materiality out of which it has developed and on which it depends. And the result is the personal union of God and man who is himself the person, Jesus Christ. In this there is discovered the personal fulfilment both of God and of man. We have the fulfilment of the personalness of God because God has achieved the expression of his purpose of love. This is the expression in conditions of materiality and history of an always perfect love so it is not a development of divine personalness. But to this we shall return in the last lecture. On the other hand we have the fulfilment of the personalness of man in the coming into existence of a perfection of relationship with God which is a personal and permanent union. But this we must consider in the seventh lecture. Meanwhile, we must be careful to note the shape of what is involved here. It is that God provides the fulfilment of his personal purposes for materiality and history by involving himself to the point where there is a personal union between transcendent personalness and derived personalness. This derived personalness is acknowledged as being wholly continuous with the impersonal stuff of the universe at large, but it is none the less asserted that such derived personalness can be lifted out of dependence on impersonal stuff, into a personal union with underived and transcendent personalness. Thus there is no denial of the immense difference between God and everything else nor of the fact that man's existence is rooted in the realm of 'everything else'. Man is clearly part of what we would call 'the universe known to science' and this is *not*

God nor continuous with God. But God unites the personal possibilities of this universe to himself in a personal union which does not destroy the distinction but achieves the personal purpose. Transcendent personalness and derived personalness are united by the immanence of the transcendent. Such is the pattern which the Chalcedonian Definition proclaims and defends. There is a union of two-foldness, of God and man, through the activity and presence of God. We do not have to choose between unique personalness and general impersonalness because God is concerned to produce and unite persons for himself out of the processes of materiality and history.

Such is the shape of the Chalcedonian Definition and its implications with regard to the questions which are of particular concern to us. Before one writes all this off as metaphysical speculation based on outmoded mythology, it is important to recall that the *structure* of this Definition was not evolved out of mere theorizing to fit in either with what men found thinkable or with what they wanted to find thinkable about themselves and the universe. This structure was evolved against the grain of the thought of the time. This thought was pessimistic about the possibilities both of materiality and of history, and strongly opposed to any idea of the involvement of God in the human and realistic way which is presupposed by the Christian definitions against the Arians and by the Definition of Chalcedon. It is a superficial mistake unsupported by a detailed study of the evidence to speak of the fourth and fifth century development of the doctrine of the Incarnation as if it were a Christianized version of a pagan and mythological theophany. The really impressive thing is that despite all the pressures upon Christians to think like that, for they were naturally men of their age as we are of ours, and despite the fact that many Christians did tend to think in terms of a God appearing as a man, the definitive pronouncements on the subject of the person of Jesus Christ steered clear of any such view and propounded a unique and very difficult doctrine. Indeed the understanding was so unique and so difficult to grasp in all its implications that, as we shall shortly see, the Church which had propounded it scarcely appreciated it and certainly often lost sight of many aspects of it.

I shall argue in the last two lectures that we are still only on the way to seeing further into its implications and applications and need in our turn to think very carefully about the understanding of God, man and the world which is demanded by this doctrine of the person of Jesus Christ. None the less it is sufficiently clear that despite all the natural pressures of the time and all the shortcomings of understanding and application, the Church of the time was led to evolve this unique statement of the *union* of God and man in and as Jesus Christ. Jesus Christ was not a theophany, that is he was not God or a God appearing as a man, a non-human being looking like and entering into the affairs of human beings. In the debates before the formulation of the Chalcedonian Definition and after it, much Christian writing and discussing came perilously close to this or actually did speak like this. But the Definition itself denies and rejects any such idea. Nor, on the other hand, is Jesus Christ to be understood simply as a man of such unique and heroic spiritual and moral stature that he is to be understood as having achieved or received God-like stature. Much modern thought in particular has felt obliged to reunderstand or misunderstand the Christian understanding of Jesus in this form. But this does not do justice to the understanding of Jesus as the Christ and Jesus Christ as Lord which formed the Church and which the Church felt bound to proclaim and defend. The discovery that Jesus was the Christ led to the discovery that he was the involvement of God and not just the attainment of man. Thus nothing but a two-fold structure understood as a personal union which had its historical expression in and as Jesus Christ was found adequate. This was necessary to hold together all the aspects of God's activity for man as it was known and understood in and through Jesus Christ. The Chalcedonian Definition is an outstanding and highly significant example of the creative and original power of the things concerning Jesus as they were experienced by the first disciples and renewed in the life-experience of the Christians who had in their turn to face the questions of the world and of themselves about the proper understanding of man's existence. The facts about Jesus required one to be clear that Jesus was unequivocally God, unequivocally man and obviously one, simply himself. Hence one must understand the world, and man in his existence in the world, on the basis of the distinct realities of God and of the derived universe and of the certainty of the union of the two in the personal purposes of God.

This unique and original understanding of the ultimate nature of things given through Jesus Christ meant that whatever the problems and difficulties which arose in the life of men nevertheless the universe was not a system hostile to or indifferent to the personal purposes which were the concern of God and of men. In the long run, although not immediately, this understanding of things cleared the way for modern science, as we shall shortly consider. But while the root possibilities of science lay dormant in the Christian approach to the universe which gradually became explicit in the first five centuries, the other most important side of our Western approach to the life of men in the world was already receiving a great deal of expansion and development in these early centuries. This, of course, was our concern for personalness and for the individual.

It was the historical Jesus Christ who presented to us the Logos of the cosmos. Thus men who shared the Christian faith in, and understanding of, Jesus Christ not only knew *that* men and the universe fitted together in and through the purpose of God, they also had some understanding of *how* this fitting together occurred. The 'how' was defined or at any rate pointed to by the actual character of the living and dying of the Jesus discovered to be the Christ and thus the Lord and so the Logos of the universe. We shall need to go into this more fully in the last two lectures. Here it is sufficient to note that while the fact that there was a Christ made it clear that there was unquestionably a God who saved men from being trapped in themselves and in the anti-human features of materiality and history, the actual nature of this Christ confirmed and re-defined the nature, activity and power of this God as being rightly understood primarily as love of a peculiar and distinctive kind. This love was the self-giving, identifying and involved love demonstrated by Jesus and commended by him through both example and commandment. It was so distinctive in its total self-identification with the loved that it was necessary to develop a little-used word, *agapē*, to refer to this love and so distinguish it from such types of love as those involved in ordinary friendship or ordinary sexual relationships which could be (although they need not be) self-centred.

Thus to know that Jesus Christ was the Logos of the cosmos and the Son of God was to know that the pattern and purpose at work in and throughout the universe was concerned with the fulfilment of each and every human-being in his or her own particularity as well as in his or her relationships. In fact the defining characteristic of every human being lies in his or her potential personal relationship to God in Jesus Christ rather than in any general or impersonal classification by status, class or any other category. Thus, while Christians have continued to fail to live up to this, it has always been a necessary implication of their response to the givenness of Jesus Christ that it should be clearly understood that in, and in relation to, ultimate reality every man and woman in his or her own particularity is of ultimate concern and of absolute worth. In the Christian view, that is to say in the way of understanding which is required by the reality of Jesus Christ, this value is rooted in the fact of God's unconditional loving concern, and ultimately to define or classify men in any other way is a mistake both of fact and of value.

Hence the Christian understanding of the true relationship between personal purposes and the processes of materiality and history makes it clear that there is, or at any rate, can be, always room for the development of the personalness of each individual. There is the possibility of freedom from the determinism of any classification or of any generalized situation which dissolves personalities into mere statistical units. This possibility is to be found in the activity of that infinitely resourceful love which is distinctively designated as *agapē*. No person need be defined or delimited by the impersonal and general features of his or her situation and existence.

But the proper understanding of the reality of Jesus Christ does not only make clear to us this freedom from the threatening determinism of the general through the possibilities of the universal scope of the love of God which liberates personalness for development and defines its infinite possibilities. There is a parallel implication that the facts of the universe are thrown open to the untrammelled investigation of science and technology. This implication arises because to discover that the Logos of the cosmos is that Jesus who is the Christ of the God who is the Lord of history is to know finally and decisively that all other divine elements in the universe have lost their rank and their power. Nothing other than that personal power who is presented in Jesus ultimately controls or underlies all that exists. You may continue to believe in demons, evil angels and even Satan, if you are conditioned to find this reasonable and not superstitious, but they are *not* 'world rulers', not built-in parts of the ordered and ordering power of the universe. Nor is it possible any longer to regard the planets or any other observable manifestation of a fixed order or regular motion in the universe as gods who control the order of the world and the life of man within the fixed pattern of their own inevitable revolutions. In fact the universe has become finally desacralized, emptied of any claim to divinity in its own right, and so free for the possibility of sanctification through personal activity. The stuff, patterns, processes and powers of the universe can now be known to be strictly neutral, neither beneficent nor malignant, and certainly not determined against men. The universe thus secularized is fully and freely open to the most rigorous probings that men can bring to bear, and the stuff and the processes of the universe lie neutrally available to be put to any end of which men can discover them to be patient. The whole of the universe is thus set free for the investigation of science and the development of technology. Because the universe is not divine, nothing bars man's free access to it. There is no numinous tabu or inhuman mystery keeping men at a distance. But, further, because it is created by the God and Father of Jesus Christ and sustained as a universe by the ordering power, the Logos, who is presented in and as Jesus Christ, the universe has to be treated authentically and seriously in its own right. It is an established and ordered given—true, a dependent given—but none the less given, and a given which proceeds from personal purposes and is open to personal purpose. Thus the universe has no divinity or personality of its own which can obtrude into or obfuscate the strict objectivity of the processes of true science, but it has its own authentic givenness which demands the strict objectivity of serious and open research and experiment and it is open to the manipulation of personal purposes.

Thus to discover that Jesus is the Christ, the Lord and the Logos of the cosmos is to discover that men are set free for the development of personalness and that the universe is set free as the material for science. The implication of the discovery that Jesus Christ is the defining datum in relation to all other data is that men have offered to them the possibilities of personalness, freedom and science. However, there is no case for, or point in, claiming that Christianity as a historical and cultural phenomenon is, as such, the 'cause' of modern science and technology. What I have been pointing out is that the things concerning Jesus do actually and intrinsically imply, demand and permit just that openness, neutrality and givenness of the stuff of the universe which is assumed in the activities of science and technology. None the less the *logical* connection between the implications of the things concerning Jesus and the required assumptions for the development of science and technology were certainly not mirrored in the *historical* relationships between organized Christianity and developing science and scientists. It is this variance between the truth as it is implied by the things concerning Jesus and the way things developed within the Christian Church in its attitude to science which we must now go on to consider.

The actual conditions of men's living in the fourth and fifth centuries of the Christian era and for many centuries beyond these were by no means favourable to the development of the whole range of potentialities which, we can now discern, were undoubtedly implied by the things concerning Jesus. Life remained, on the whole, 'nasty, brutish and short' and the Christian message of liberation for infinite development tended inevitably to concentrate on the aspect of the liberation of the individual personality for the infinite development of the relationship with God through the relationship of the individuals with God. Thus Christianity in the West tended to be centred more and more on the freeing of the individual from his burden of sin, while in the East the living heart of Christian spirituality was to be found in the pursuit of that ever-closer identification of the soul with God which led to 'deification', to the transfusion of the whole life of the believer with the very life of God. And the path to deification was by way of the *askēsis*, the discipline and training of withdrawal. Of course, such generalizations are gross over-simplifications. In the West from Augustine's

City of God onwards there was much concern with society, the state, and with innumerable problems of men's lives and the context of men's lives, while the East, as can be seen from iconography as well as from spirituality, always retained the vision of *cosmic* redemption, of Christ as the last Adam and head of the redeemed race of men and of the eventual penetration of the universe by the uncreated glory of God. None the less, in practice Christianity was not much concerned with the liberation and development of the natural powers in the universe—indeed there was no technique available to bring about such liberation.

These techniques, which are now so splendidly open to us in wide measure and which have every prospect of further vast increases in range, began to be produced as modern science developed from, say, the sixteenth century onwards, with its greatest acceleration in our time. But Christianity, having settled down into its mediaeval moulds, was largely unable to 'take' the strictly neutral and secular approach to everything in the universe (including eventually, man in so far as he is homogeneous with the rest of the universe), which is the essence of the scientific approach and which gives it its liberating and creative effect. Thus scientific developments were frequently seen, and indeed still are seen, as threats to the Christian religion. In this we have what is perhaps the most outstanding and the most disastrous example of the way in which the Christian religion—i.e. the alleged following of Jesus Christ as organized, practised and institutionalized—again and again gets off-centre from its true and only *raison d'être*—Jesus Christ himself. For Jesus Christ has neutralized and secularized the processes and stuff of the universe—albeit in relation to the purposes of God. But in so far as the Church pushed outside itself the Christian truth which lies in the scientific approach to the universe and to man in the universe, it is in no position to lord it over scientists who then proceeded to push out the other side of Christian truth about the universe and man—which is that all can properly be understood and handled only in relation to God. Scientists may have brought about the apparent exclusion of God, but if there is any point in allotting *blame* for this then we would probably do better to apportion it to the Church who attempted to confine the God and Father of Jesus Christ to the so-called sacred when Jesus Christ himself had already abolished the separation of sacred and secular *within* the universe. He had, of course, not destroyed the distinction between God and everything created, but that is something to which we shall return much later in the argument.

The most important effect of this hostility or, at best, lack of enthusiasm, in the relations between the Church and developing science is to be seen most clearly not in the contributors to the so-called war between religion and science but in those who continued to believe that Christianity and science somehow went together, for they affected the combination or co-existence in a disastrous and fundamentally un-Christian manner.

Descartes may be taken as symptomatic of the resultant false move, the more so as his influence contributed much to the development and ramification of this falsity. What Descartes did was to assume, and work on the basis of, a dichotomy between spirit and matter. Matter was the stuff of the universe which was the proper subject matter of the deterministic-type study of science. Spirit was, so to speak, the soul-stuff which was related to, and capable of, relationship with God.

The relationship of spirit to matter was a complete mystery. One just had to assume a parallelism between, say, the material movements open to the study of science which were involved in the muscular raising of an arm, and the spiritual activity which was the willing of the raising of the arm for the purpose of striking an angry blow. Men had to be thought of as physical organisms with a mysteriously parallel psychical life. And the distinction between the transcendent God and everything created became thought of in a way analogous to the dichotomy between spirit and matter within the universe. Spirit was God's realm and matter was the realm of science. The relationship between the two realms was a taken-for-granted parallelism which was also an insoluble mystery. For instance, how did the (spiritual) mind apprehend the reality of (material) objects? Locke, Hume, Berkeley and Kant all gave different and equally theoretical answers to this 'mystery'. Or again, how could the materially determined human organism be spiritually free? The relationship between the spiritual aspect of man and the material world had become an insoluble problem which had replaced the mystery of man's experience of the relationship between God and his creation. The effect of all this was to make one's belief in, commitment to, and practice of science one thing, and one's belief in God another.

God was the truly spiritual, who was not involved in or concerned with the universe as the subject of science. He could be known spiritually only. Thus if one were a Cartesian, one could know him inwardly by the clarity of the idea of God which reflection presented to one's mind. If one were a Kantian, one could know him only transcendentally when the wholly unique intuition of the moral imperative took one from the realm of the phenomenal to the wholly separate realm of freedom and immortality. Or if one followed the more deliberately theological solution of Schleiermacher, one apprehended God through the feeling of absolute dependence which was to be most carefully distinguished from knowledge, which gave one access to the scientific realm, and moral sense, which gave one access to the ethical. 'Religion', says Schleiermacher triumphantly, 'resigns all claim on science and morality'.

But in such a dichotomous situation it is clearly only a matter of time before we come to the obvious conclusion of Laplace concerning God. We have no need of *that* hypothesis. For as Kant himself pointed out against Descartes, clarity of idea implies nothing whatever about actual existence. And innumerable scientists in their pragmatism have outweighed Kant himself. The noumenal, the realm of freedom, immortality and God is, by Kant's own account, in no way known in the way in which scientific data is known. And the weight and effectiveness of scientific data is such that it is the scientific way of knowing which calls the tune as to what knowledge is. And in that case, where is the Kantian realm of the noumenal? And as to feelings of absolute dependence and judgements of value, are not feelings and judgements all our attitudes pure and simple? The fact that we have a godly attitude says nothing about the existence of God. Thus it turns out that theology is purely evaluative anthropology—the way in which we have hitherto expressed our understanding of the value of man. And Jesus Christ, if he is to be retained for a unique role at all, turns out to be the outstanding example of *our* understanding of the world and man. (For the Hegelian the realization of Spirit, for the existentialist the example of authentic existence and so on.)

When the realm of God was separated from the realm of science, it was supposed that the realm of God could be retained by making a corresponding dichotomy within man's approach to the universe and separating out the realm of spirit and the realm of matter. But the effect of this latter dichotomy in the history of thought was to reduce God to a hypothesis, a moral command or a feeling. Hence the way was open to discovering that we have no need of the hypothesis and that values and feelings are simply and decisively human. This prepared the way for the discovery that God is dead and Jesus, who strangely continues to exercise some compelling power for some, is then, if he is anything, the glory of man. We must leave it to the next lecture to face the evidence that if God is dead then man is dying.

VI

The Loss of Man

THE CHALCEDONIAN DEFINITION of the person of Jesus Christ stood for the belief and the assertion that the God who was transcendentally responsible for the existence of the universe and for the production of personal purpose out of the stuff of materiality and out of the events of history had become immanent in, and a part of, materiality and history, for the sake of his personal concern. This he had achieved by being the person whose name is Jesus, but not in such a way that the Creator was dissolved into a creature nor in such a way that the validity and authenticity of the creature was done away with or distorted in any way by the presence and power of the Creator. Thus it was asserted as literally true that materiality and history are capable of being led to produce an embodied and dependent personalness which is capable of union with transcendent and underived personalness. The homogeneous material universe is rightly understood as related to personal purposes because it finds its fulfilment in the natural organism man who is capable of receiving personal union with the transcendentally personal God.

So man with his personal and spiritual potentialities is not to be set over against the impersonal, indifferent and material universe of which he is none the less also mysteriously and seemingly tragically a part. Rather, a man is a wholly natural part of the universe which proceeds from, and is being moved towards, personal purposes. In man, the personal possibilities of the universe emerge and are brought to fulfilment by being brought into union with the personalness of the God from and for whose personal purposes the universe exists. Thus there is no dichotomy in man or between man in some particular aspect of his being and the rest of the universe. Man is a homogeneous, although not yet fully developed, whole and the particular pattern and structure which constitutes man is itself a pattern and structure within and homogeneous with the pattern and structure of the whole universe. The *distinction* with which the Chalcedonian Definition is concerned is the same distinction with which the whole tradition of biblical theism is concerned. This is the distinction between the totality of the universe, the sum-total of everything that is 'created', and the God and Creator who is transcendent to and other than the universe.

But this distinction is not a *dichotomy*. God and the universe are not kept apart in some inexplicable parallelism wherein the material events of the universe have some shadowy set of spiritual and divine parallels. God and the universe in their respective distinctivenesses, in their two distinct 'natures', are closely involved, although not confused. This involvement is throughout the product of the untrammelled will and purpose of God. The transcendence of God remains untouched. He is in no way dependent for his being God on either the existence or the events of the universe. But the universe depends for its existence and its fulfilment entirely on God. This is the first involvement. There is no dichotomy between God and the universe, because God is in the closest possible touch with the universe as its originating, continuing and consummating cause. The second involvement lies in the presence and activity of God in the processes of materiality and in the events of history to produce a development whereby there shall emerge personal beings capable of a personal knowledge of and response to himself. This involvement includes also the presence and activity whereby these personal beings do actually become aware of the personal reality who is God. The first involvement corresponds very broadly to that which would come in traditional theology under the heading of Creation, while the second comes, again very broadly, under the heading of Revelation. The third involvement is the personal presence of God in and as Jesus Christ. This is fully personal in the sense that God is present in his personalness, that Jesus is a fully human person, and in the sense that the union of God and man is the person, Jesus Christ. Thus Creation, Revelation and Incarnation all speak of the involvement of the distinctive God in the universe for the fulfilment of his personal purposes. These purposes are so personal that the absolute distinction whereby God in his wholly unique and independent Godness transcends everything else is itself transcended or fulfilled in a perfect union with the personalness that has emerged from the dependent and derived 'everything else' which is so distinct from God.

All this implies that any Christianity which is continuous with the reality and revelation of Jesus Christ must be deeply and fully conerned with the widest possible exploration of every feature of the universe and of every opportunity and possibility which it offers to the personal activities and concerns of men. But, as we know only too well and as I discussed briefly in the last lecture, the exploration of the universe and development of its practical possibilities through science and technology have very largely been seen as hostile to Christianity both from within and from without the Christian faith. There can be no doubt whatever that this is a mistake and it is a mistake which has done far more than threaten the continuing existence of the Church. It has led to a threat to the continuing existence of the humanity of man.

I have used a reference to Descartes to draw attention to the dichotomy which has characterized modern man's understanding of himself and of his existence in the world in relation both to the development of science and technology and in relation to his knowledge and understanding of God. It is most important to take full note that it is 'dichotomy' which is the correct word here and not the word 'distinction'. For there is no question of the involvement of two existences or natures which are distinct but which have a purposeful and personal relationship leading to a union. There is no involvement of mind and matter. There is only the theoretically assumed mystery which is really only a mystifying and insoluble puzzle of how two totally and necessarily (by definition) distinct types of existence none the less co-exist in parallel and perform a series of shadow dances.

This is a pretty desperate expedient to try and hold on to the materialistic and deterministic side of things on the one hand, and to the free, human and spiritual on the other. But thinkers like Descartes and Kant and, indeed, their successors down to our own time, were in a pretty desperate situation. It seemed clear to them that science and technology advance by methods that are necessarily neutral, impersonal and deterministic. It was also clear that if such methods extend exhaustively to everything that can in any sense be said to exist then the essentially human, spiritual and lively aspects of our existence as free or potentially free persons are done away with. Further, there was no assistance or illumination from theology or from officially Christian thinking to baptize this situation as a whole into an understanding which could see the neutral and deterministic material of science as clearly within a transcendent personal purpose. Rather, the Church fell back on its own sacred realm as over against the powerful growing secular and scientific realm by which it was increasingly threatened. Since many of the thinkers who knew the power and authenticity of science wanted to go on believing in God, and since all of them wanted to go on believing in man, they were forced back on an essentially atheistic way of conceiving the relationship between the material, impersonal and deterministic aspect and the spiritual, personal and human aspect of existence as known to men. Further, this relationship is not only essentially atheistic, it is not even in reality a relationship.

To preserve the full force of both aspects of existence, a dichotomy was assumed between them. This would keep science free from the confusion of the personal, and the personal free from the stranglehold of determinism, while God was left to go on being God as long as men had a clear idea of him. But what kept the dichotomy together, and *a fortiori*, what kept God attached to any part of it? The last part of this question is not mere rhetoric, because the original perpetrators of, and thinkers about, the dichotomy, such as Descartes and Berkeley, assumed that it was God who kept the dichotomy together. The situation of existence was in this dichotomous form because God had so arranged it and so sustained it. But God does not long survive when his status becomes that of a hypothesis which needs no explanation in order to enable men to hold a hypothesis which does. (One might be inclined to assume that if God were godly he would not care to survive under such circumstances!) Even Kant's attempt to, so to speak, skewer together the two sides of the dichotomy, now known as the phenomenal and the noumenal, by the self-evident intuition of the categorical imperative, and then to continue God in the rôle of guarantor that this Kantian intuition was in fact an intuition of reality, did not do much to prolong the life of the God-hypothesis. As the transcendent other had been in effect excluded from any purposeful participation in the affairs of materiality and history which was where the effective knowledge and the effective experience of men lay, God was in fact dying, although one has to wait for Nietzsche definitely to proclaim the triumphant and the tragic fact of his death.

But with God out of the way, what then becomes of the dichotomy? It is left in its nakedness, to be seen as not even a relationship. It is possible to make sense of, and go on believing in, a relationship of personal purpose which exists between two distinct realities or natures of which at least one is personal and purposeful. Thus, if one has grounds for believing in a transcendent and personal God, then it is perfectly possible to make sense of the notion of his having a relationship of purpose and activity with anything completely distinct from him, with inert and impersonal matter as well as with active and personal creatures. But it is not possible to make sense of a relationship between what are held to be two distinct existences or natures like mind and matter and, indeed, no one ever has. For mind and matter are, *ex hypothesi*, two dichotomous aspects of, or existences within, the total existence of the universe which includes man who, of course, shares in this dichotomy. But as far as our observations and experience go, neither 'mind' nor 'matter' are personal and purposeful existences. The personal and purposeful existence known to us is man who, already, on the theory, *consists* of the dichotomy. Thus there is nothing to relate or hold together the dichotomy which was in any case set up precisely because of the difficulties, dangers and quite probable impossibility of the relationship. Man has thus become an insoluble problem to himself. He has, indeed, an impossible picture of himself.

Hegel attempted to solve the problem by promoting mind in the mysterious form of *Geist*, or Spirit, to a purposeful although not a personal and, in the traditional sense, not a transcendent reality. But it is clear that Hegelianism is purely theoretical thinking designed to answer problems which the history of thought has simply generated for itself, and that it never comes down to dealing with actual historicity or materiality. Hegel and his followers thought that this was precisely the strength of his sytem. Pressure of space and time forces me to assume that you will agree with me that this flight from the actual realm of particular materiality and historicity into the doubtfully existent realm of the general and so called 'spiritual' is a form of escapism which has already given up hope of any realistic solution to the problem that man is to himself. There is a further fact which makes it decisively clear that Hegelianism is nothing but mythology, i.e. a theory which tells a tale about man and the nature of his existence in the world without any sufficient anchorage in the actual stuff of the world and of history. This is that Hegelianism can be simply stood on its head to produce Marxism, wherein the rôle of the purposeful but immanent and impersonal *Geist*, or spirit, is taken over by the apparently purposeful but most certainly impersonal dialectic of the *material* process.

In fact Hegelianism and Marxism show that the dichotomy of spirit and matter cannot be held. Either spirit or matter has to be promoted to the rôle of God, although the transcendent, personal God of the Bible is assumed to be unthinkable and therefore dead, and so this rôle has to be played by an immanent and impersonal force for whose existence there is, and can be, no sufficient evidence and which, indeed, would never have been thought of if it had not seemed necessary to find a thinkable substitute for the God of the Bible. But you cannot think up substitutes for God. If he is dead then he is dead. And with his death there is the decisive collapse of all mythologies which cling outmodedly to the view that materiality and historicity have a purposeful pattern which can be perceived by those who receive through secular prophets such as Hegel or Marx the clue to the inner although impersonal 'Logos' of the historical process. Purpose and pattern are a feature of personalness. Since there is no transcendent personalness, there is no overall purpose or pattern. There is not even open to us the freedom of the acceptance of necessity in becoming a conscious part of the dialectical process. For it is simply a myth of the human imagination that there is such a process. As far as our observation goes there is no process—only processes.

Marxism may fight an old-fashioned rearguard action, and certainly in its political effects it remains a force to be reckoned with—but not as a philosophy purveying truth about the world and about man's existence in the world. With the death of God it is clear that there is no Logos of the cosmos; that indeed, as Bertrand Russell has pointed out, we are not really entitled to use an expression like 'cosmos' or 'universe', with its implication that we are talking about a structured whole. What we face in arriving at our own self-understanding is the recognition of the reality of fragmentation. There is no sense to be made of anything, other than the sense which we can each of us make for ourselves. We are left with the problem of what is the relationship of that in us which wishes to make sense to the senselessness of everything else, including the rest of ourselves, but we know that this is both a problem and a senseless one. We are thus finally and definitely clear that we are an insoluble problem to ourselves.

There appear to be current two significant reactions to this existential situation of which the second has two distinctive forms. The first is to turn to various forms of Oriental monism or simply to various techniques of escape, yoga and the like, which can be detached from their attendant and consequent philosophy and be used very like drugs. We are an insoluble problem to ourselves and therefore we must practice techniques which enable us to cease to be aware of ourselves or even follow out a philosophy and practice which will ultimately set us free from being selves at all. Clearly this is, in the most literal sense, the absolute contradiction of that direction and activity of the self which has produced science and technology. The thinking, analyzing, organizing and practising self and all its achievements of knowledge about the universe and consequent power to better so many of the aspects of man's life in the universe has got to be eschewed and got rid of. We are to return to the oblivion of the womb, of not being a self, and to turn our backs decisively on all the achievements, possibilities and responsibilities of human living in a universe patient of scientific and technological manipulation. Such a personal choice, to deny and reject the opportunities and responsibilities of being a person, is clearly an acknowledgement of the total bankruptcy of man. The point of being human is to cease to be human. But to say that man is totally bankrupt is to choose to deny that the human achievements of science and technology are to count as achievements at all. But this is to make an arbitrary choice as to what counts as determining evidence about the human predicament on the basis of an already arrived at pessimism about the truth of the human predicament. There is, and can be, no evidence which compels the conclusion that all human thinking, achievements and possibilities are nothing but valueless illusions. Any philosophy and practice which alleges this must proceed from the decision that it is not humanly possible to cope with being human, so that what must be repudiated is humanness, and it must then read the evidence of the human condition in that light.

The fact that men are turning to such pessimistic and personality-denying practices and philosophies at a time when scientific and technological possibilities have reached an unprecedented level is one important symptom of the way in which the opposing, or at any rate the separating, of the realm of the scientific and material, and the realm of personal and spiritual, produces a situation in which the personal is repudiated and so the scientific becomes wholly futile. This is doubtless in the logic of the situation in which we have forced ourselves to the non-sense that we are insoluble and meaningless problems to ourselves, but in logic a false proposition can imply any conclusion whatever. Here we have one piece of non-sense producing or at any rate supporting another piece of non-sense.

The other symptomatic and rather commoner reaction to the awareness that the human situation exists in the face of fragmentation is the various forms of existentialism. These would seem to fall into two main types in which the predominant reaction to the realized nonsensicality of the human situation is either nausea in the face of the Absurd or courage in the face of despair. Nausea can lead to complete cynicism, hectic sensuality and meaningless triviality. This response is reflected in not a few plays and novels. Here it is clear enough that man is dead although he is not yet quite able to lie down. With courage in the face of despair, humanness is somehow maintained until the evident sentence of death is finally executed. But the protest has no final point. The sense which we can make for ourselves and the values which we can create for ourselves scarcely seem

to burn brightly enough to illuminate humanity more than flicker-
ingly. The main characteristic of the whole philosophy and approach
is one of protest. But it is a negative protest against the whole human
condition, not a positive protest against anti-humane features in that
condition which are to be striven against for the sake of a deeper
humanness. Man complains bitterly against his condition, but there
is no-one to complain to and nothing to be gained by complaining.

Once again we have a complete contrast with the other side of the
life of modern man, with the spirit of science and of technology.
Here one does not complain. One diagnoses problems and works out
how to programme solutions. There would thus seem to be a good
deal of plausibility in the view that the Cartesian dichotomy has
either itself led, or is symptomatic of a more general approach to the
life of the world which has led, to a real and very destructive split in
man's understanding of and hopes for himself. When operating on
the scientific and material side he is optimistic and purposeful. When
reflecting on the human and spiritual side he is pessimistic and
hopeless, so much so that he is prepared in one way or another to
write off the achievements of his scientific side and his own personalness with them.

But surely this is absurd—and straightforwardly so, not in any
technical existentialist sense? (We may note in passing that this
might be true but that logic does not prevent men practising
absurdity if they have strong enough existential reasons for doing
so.) After all, the achievements of men on what I have called the
'scientific side' are achievements of what must be called the human
and spiritual side of man, if we are going to contrast material and
spiritual in any way. Scientific optimism is as much the product of
humanness as is existential despair. Is there not, therefore, a simple
solution to the situation in which we find that we are insoluble
problems to ourselves? Let us eschew existential problems and, *a
fortiori*, the escapism of monistic withdrawal, and concentrate on the
pursuit and practice of science and technology.

Now let us assume that this total putting on one side of existential
and undermining questions is possible. (I do not for a moment
believe that it is, has been or ever will be, but so many people who
pride themselves on being scientific are so insistent on ignoring a

whole range of the plainly observable features of human living for the sake of what they persist in calling scientific and empirical theories, that I am prepared to make the assumption for the sake of the argument.) We do not then ask existential questions, we concentrate on the pursuit of science and technology in order to avoid the pessimism so destructive of humanness and personality which we have been considering. What *then* happens to humanness and personalness? They are clearly threatened with even more certain extinction. For science and technology have, as such, no means of recognizing or reckoning with humanness and personalness. These reside in the particularity of individuals, however much they are built up by and from the individual's roots in both his physical and his social and human environment. But the impersonal, neutral and necessarily generalizing techniques of science and technology cannot possibly recognize individuals, still less personal individuals constituted as such by their own unique particularity and personalness. Social and human engineering and social and human science, in the sense that human individuals and human society are the *objects* of science and engineering, come very close to being contradictions in terms unless there is an awareness of the existential dimension of human personalness, which then prevents them from being purely scientific and technological. Existentialism may recognize that man in his humanness is dying, but science, if it indulges in unscientific optimism about its total capacity to deal with the problems of man, might much more easily kill off man's humanness without even noticing it.

I think it is quite sufficiently clear that man's humanness and personalness is threatened with death, and that not only in the sense that every individual human person must die. The whole of what has hitherto been glimpsed as being involved in a lively humanness and in a purposeful and particular personalness is threatened on the one hand by the enervating and consciously pointless complaining of a pessimistic existentialism, and on the other by an over-optimistic scientism. This latter supposes that science and technology can solve all human ills by statistical and generalizing methods which of necessity dissolve the particular qualities of humanness into the general qualities of materiality. Many men have lost their nerve to be human, while others have too much nerve on a front which is too narrow to have room for all that is involved in being human.

Must we then fall back on the position that human personalness is indeed always under threat, that it has no ultimate place in the scheme of things (which is in any case not a scheme) and that we must summon up what courage we can in the face of absurdity and despair to keep alive what personalness we may to whatever degree we may? And shall we find enough resources to do this in the face of all the changes and chances of humanity on the one hand and in the face of the all-conquering prestige of science on the other? Moreover, why try?

Here we might consider two things, one in the form of a further question, the other a statement. The question is, 'Why should science, which is the product of human-beings, threaten human-ness?'. The statement is that Jesus Christ has made it clear that human personalness is a focus of reality which is at all costs to be maintained and developed. Let us proceed from the statement and return to the question.

When we are considering the Cartesian dichotomy, the Kantian categorical imperative, the Hegelian doctrine of Spirit, the Marxist view of dialectical materialism, Oriental forms of monism, or existential pessimism, we are considering theories which men have formulated about the total nature of things. This is as true of existentialism as of any other philosophy. These theories are formed because men choose particular features that they are aware of in the world and in their own existence as being of decisive significance for their understanding of the totality of existence. On the basis of this choice they erect their structure which is supposed to embrace the whole of existence, to give one one's complete and exhaustive picture. Thus all these philosophies, or rather all the philosophies which contain the features I have referred to, are exercises in metaphysical mythology or mythological metaphysics. They purport to give decisively true pictures of reality. In fact they are tales which men have chosen to tell with more or less reason, and with a greater or lesser degree of articulation, about the way they think reality should be apprehended and responded to.

Science can be turned into such a metaphysical mythology as

well. This happens when it is claimed that reality in the sense of all that exists and all that counts as existing in the long run is co-extensive with that which is or which can be investigated by science. When this happens, when for instance a biologist authoritatively assures us that man is essentially and definitively a biological organism, or a psychologist decisively claims that personality is really a matter of psycho-dynamics, then we have passed from science properly so called to metaphysical mythology. There is no absolutely decisive evidence, certainly no strictly scientific evidence, for seeing man or the universe as wholly within the framework of any particular science or of all the sciences. The person who demands or recommends that we should do so is simply registering the choice which he has made. He has decided to take scientific evidence as *the* decisive clue in the understanding of man and the world and to build his complete picture accordingly. It should perhaps be scarcely necessary to reiterate that this is not a scientific procedure. Total frameworks are not the products of scientific investigation but of human choice and imagination, including the total framework which consists in maintaining that there is no such thing, but only meaningless fragments.

Any framework, any metaphysical theory which has proved influential, has done so because it was not entirely arbitrary, or simply *mere* imagination and choice. The choice of the basis was clearly influenced by recognizable features in men's then current life and understanding, and the imagination which erected the structure was clearly guided by insights related to the same things. Thus powerfully influential metaphysical theories are not arbitrary. But however powerful and plausible they are, they are never final or bound to give the truth about things. Thus we need never be tied to any theory or philosophy save by our own choice.

We may choose to see ourselves and the world in some particular framework. We may say that we refuse to do anything of the kind and thus either be unaware that we are conforming to the prevalent spirit of the age or else, and much more rarely, be setting out to practice the impossible and be a consistent nihilist. Or we may choose Jesus Christ as our decisive point of reference and our defence against being shut up in any necessarily partial and inevitably misleading theory whatever. For Jesus Christ has the advantage over every theory that he has happened and was not just thought up. Much has been thought about him and Christians have again and again tried to destroy him by shutting him up in theories. But as I have tried to show in the first half of these lectures, I would claim that the essential insights which Jesus Christ makes available to us are derived from his happenedness and givenness and that it is he and the facts about him which control the truly Christian understanding of things. And as I shall try to show in the last two lectures, this understanding is not and never can be a theory which provides a frame which embraces everything. Rather it is, and must always be, open to new and hitherto unknown possibilities. In this I am convinced that true Christianity is precisely the same as true science. Both are required to be totally open to whatever is authentically given in each situation. This is no mere coincidence. For it is Jesus Christ who definitively makes it clear that the universe is truly open to truly scientific investigation.

With regard to our particular dilemma about why or how to go on being concerned with human personalness, I would simply say at this stage that my answer is that the happenedness of Jesus decisively reinforces the intuition which I discussed at length in the first lecture that our concern is with persons and that this concern can be resourcefully pursued. This is the main subject of the next lecture. With regard to the question why science, which is the product of human beings, should threaten humanness, I would now answer that this is so because with the exclusion of God, which is at least as much the fault of the Church as of the scientist, men lost the possibility of uniting the basically and originally impersonal and material resources of the universe with the personal purposes which *under God* became the decisive and distinctive concern of men. Thus the personal union of Chalcedon degenerates into the impersonal dichotomy of Descartes, and man becomes an insoluble problem to himself. As a result man either loses his wholeness by seeking to find his humanity in a desperate defiance quite apart from, and contrary to, science, as in existentialism, or loses his human personalness by succumbing to the generality and impersonality of science.

Thus at present we find man concentrated on his existential predicament. The result seems to be to bring him near to despairing of his humanness. As I pointed out, while European thought was on the way to this conclusion Feuerbach remarked that all theology was really anthropology. I propose that we should take up this very significant remark and see what becomes of the existential predicament of man if, and with the help of Jesus Christ, we see whether we may reconsider all anthropology as theology. Certainly the reduction of theology to anthropology was a prelude to reducing anthropology to absurdity. If we have grounds for re-understanding anthropology as theology, we may yet have hope that we can be rescued from the Absurd.

VII

Real Man

MAN IS NOT absurd. It would be nearer the truth to say that he is divine. But if he is substituted for God, or if he denies God, then he is nothing. Theology can be plausibly reduced to anthropology because in reality man is in the image of God and depends for the fulfilment of his humanness on the transcendent and personal reality of God. As the image of God, man is truly human. Once, however, man effectively rejects the idea that he is in the image of God and decides that God is simply the shadow of man, then his essential humanness is at the mercy of the massive impersonality and indifference of a godless and, *ipso facto*, inhuman universe. This absurd situation arises because of the refusal or failure to understand that all anthropology is inevitably theology. Man to be man requires God, because God is the cause as he is the end of the emergence of man.

But what grounds have we for maintaining that anthropology is ultimately and inevitably theology? Why is my foregoing paragraph not just one more piece of metaphysical mythology whereby I choose to defend myself from the absurdity of man by sheltering behind the fantasy of God? The grounds for maintaining the inevitable extension of anthropology into theology are two-fold.

Firstly, we have seen how the death of God strikes a mortal blow at the humanness and personalness of man. But can we really and reasonably lose faith in human personalness? It may be urged that the apprehension of personalness and of the uniqueness of the dimension of the person which I was particularly concerned to point to in my first lecture is simply a set of epiphenomenal feelings which happen to have arisen among a certain group of organisms which happen to have been thrown up with this characteristic reaction-pattern. Thus it could be argued that the apprehension of personalness is no more significant of what reality is like in the end than, say, the fact that, as far as can be ascertained, most normal people react to a certain wavelength of light by seeing a colour called 'blue'. We happen to 'see a colour we call blue', whatever that means, and we happen 'to react to personalness', whatever *that* means. Or perhaps the situation would be even better characterized by pointing out that some people find blue a wonderful colour, others loathe it, and some are colour-blind. Why should we suppose that the apprehension of personalness is decisively different from this sort of thing?

There are at least three reasons, even at this level of the argument, for maintaining that the apprehension of personalness is decisively different from a reaction consisting in a set of epiphenomenal feelings. The first one is intuitive; I have already dwelt on it at some length and I must refer you back to it. You must take a long, hard and honest look at what is involved for you in being a person in relation to persons and see if you can reasonably and consistently commit yourself to the view that what is involved here is nothing but a reaction like excitement at red or boredom at green. The second reason for seeing more in the apprehension of personalness than mere feelings is what I would refer to as the observable mystery of persons. By this I mean the logical and practical impossibility of fitting human beings as persons into any single framework. This I have touched on in the first lecture, and said a good deal about in lectures V and VI. There is a clearly observable way in which human beings can and do transcend their environments and are recognizably different in their behaviour and their effects from non-human features of that environment. This is, of course, by no means always the case, but the cases where human personalness is recognizable are quite sufficient to give strong support to the view that in apprehending personalness we are becoming aware of a distinctive feature in things and not just having a feeling. Men are homogeneous with the rest of material creation, but it is an observable and objective fact that as human and personal they demand to be treated differently.

We may reasonably hold, therefore, that in observing personalness we are observing an objective and significant feature of things as they are, the more so when we take into account our third consideration, which is that of the moral and practical effects of distinctively human living. The personal qualities of human beings, especially of notable human beings at their most personal and individual, have made their mark on what can be done with, and what can be done within, the possibilities of materiality and history. The achievements of art, of technology and of science are indisputable, even if their evaluation can be a matter of debate. Thus we have very strong grounds for holding that in apprehending personalness we are apprehending some real feature in the emerging nature of things which is of particular significance. Faith in human personalness, therefore, is a very reasonable faith which has considerable claim to inform, if not direct, our reasoning.

We have, in fact, reasonable grounds for believing that anthropology ought not to be reducible to absurdity. Since this is so and since also we have seen that the elimination of theology from anthropology was related to and relatable to the reduction of anthropology to absurdity, we may at least entertain the idea that in fact anthropology does imply and involve theology. We have very strong, even if not decisive, grounds for retaining our faith in man. It may very well be, therefore, that we have equally strong grounds for hoping that we ought to retain our faith in God. Man is not dead. This may well be because God is not dead either.

It is important to be quite clear that this is not a 'God of the gaps' argument. That is to say, we are not suggesting faith in the liveliness of God in order to fill a gap which is said to be visible in the liveliness of man. The argument does not arise from finding a weakness in the situation of man which is then exploited into a gap into which God may be fitted as a cosmic anodyne and an anthropological placebo. The argument arises from the strength of the case for continuing to have faith in the liveliness of man. Man is not dead. Is there not something of the divine in his liveliness?

I would certainly claim that a careful inspection of, and reflection on, the most characteristically human aspects of the human situation provide much that can legitimately be taken as evidence of the divineness of man. This divineness is derived. Moreover, it is a divineness which is not only derived but also largely potential only,

for it is the divineness of a creature who is emerging out of materiality and history as a personal pattern capable of forming relationships
which are ultimately fulfillable in a relationship of union with the
uncreated and transcendent divinity of the true God himself. The
simplest way of referring to this quality of incipient and potential
divineness which is characteristic of that which is most human in
man, is to make use of the biblical notion that man is in the image of
God. He has built into the emerging pattern which is characteristically human a reflection of the freedom, transcendence and creati-
vity which is to be glimpsed in the divine personalness of God. Thus
I would summarize the first main argument for maintaining the
inevitable extension of anthropology into theology as lying in the
evidence of the liveliness of man despite the threat of absurdity
with which the alleged death of God has faced him. We may
reasonably continue to have faith in man, and this demands that
we re-examine the position with regard to faith in God. I have
interpolated into that argument an anticipatory comment of my
own which is that it is in fact in the liveliness of man that we see
evidences of that derived divineness which characterizes the reality
of man and which is best referred to by understanding man as being
in the image of God. He reflects divine qualities and is heading for
union with the divine personalness who is God.

But this particular comment of mine is intruding into the argument concerning the first ground for maintaining that anthropology
is inescapably theology something that is properly an extension of
the second ground. It may be reasonable to hold on to faith in man,
and some may even admit that it is reasonable to go on from faith in
man to reconsidering faith in God. But there is nothing absolutely
compelling about this reasoning, and some will certainly hold that it
is not really reasonable at all. I believe I have alleged reasonable
grounds for claiming human personalness as an objective feature of
reality as we know it, and for the claim that this feature of reality
deserves to be taken as a significant clue to an authentic and valid
approach to reality as a whole. But, as we have had occasion to
observe at various points throughout the lectures, men have been
confronted, and we are today confronted, with counter-claims about
the proper understanding of reality and our existence which some

hold to be equally reasonable and others hold to overwhelm all reason. We have, therefore, to be clear that the second ground for holding that anthropology is inevitably theology is not a set of reasons, but the givenness of a personal happening, that is to say the givenness of Jesus Christ.

Jesus was a particular man who lived out a particular pattern of life under particular circumstances. He happened. Through the happenings which focused on his personal particularity, he was recognized as the Christ of God, and from this it was seen that the shape of his happenedness presented in a form embodied in materiality and history the shape of the Logos of the cosmos. This recognition of Jesus as the Christ and of Jesus Christ as Lord and Logos is, of course, the recognition of faith. I have tried to indicate the type of grounds on which the Christian believer is entitled and, indeed, obliged, to assert both to himself and to all believers or unbelievers that the recognition of faith is recognition and not composition. The shape of the happenedness of Jesus is an historical given which does set forth the shape of the Kingdom of God and therefore the shape of the personal pattern and purpose which is at work behind, in and beyond the patterns and processes of materiality and history. This is not a theory, but the faithful perception through experience and experiment wholly involved in things and events, of the pattern of the purposes of the God who transcends materiality and history. The decisive ground for being clear that anthropology implies theology is that the shape of the happenedness of the life of the man Jesus is wholly orientated towards God, and the significance of the life of the man Jesus is discovered to be the pattern of the purposes of God. The facts of the liveliness of man legitimately raise the question of the continuing livingness of God. The shape of the givenness of Jesus Christ answers the question both as to the reality of the livingness of God and as to the nature of the liveliness of man. For the rest of this lecture we must concentrate on Jesus Christ as the definition, demonstration and declaration of the reality of man, leaving to the last lecture some consideration of the witness of Jesus Christ to the truth about God.

Since Jesus Christ was a particular man who lived his own distinctive life his happenedness had its own particular shape. The discovery that Jesus was the Christ meant that this distinctive, particular shape of his life became definitive for the understanding of the realities of man's life and of the realities of God's dealings with men. This becomes immediately and importantly obvious at the very first stages of the life of Christianity by the way in which the shape of the life of Jesus demands, and indeed constitutes, a re-definition of the notion of 'Messiah'.

The fact that Jesus is the Messiah, the Christ, decisively de-mythologizes and universalizes the biblical and Jewish understanding of God, the pattern of his purposes and the methods of his activity. The build-up to the recognition of Jesus as the Christ I have already discussed, and I have given some indication of the way in which the notion of the Christ is related to that of the Kingdom of God and of how that notion was developed out of the experience of those people who became the Jews and was used by them as an expression of their faith in the consistency of the character and activity of the God they had come to know. Naturally, the whole set of ideas which included the picture of the Kingdom of God and the expectation of the Christ was imprecise, had at some points conflicting features, and contained a number of mythological elements. That is to say, a more or less consistent story was told about God and his dealings with men based on selected incidents and experiences in the past, which then passed over into a story which predicted the future of God's dealings with men.

With the discovery that Jesus is the Christ this story is discovered to come true in a twofold sense. Firstly, the story is vindicated as having its truth value rooted in the realities of materiality and history as known to men, out of which men have developed as men and in which men live as men and must strive to be human. I have already discussed this truth-establishing aspect of the discovery that Jesus is the Christ. For our present purposes it is the second side of the coming true of the story in Jesus as the Christ which is important. We now know on the basis of event and experience what is the true way of telling the story. Jesus who is the Christ is the way God acts. Jesus Christ is the visible embodiment of the pattern and powers of the Kingdom. If you want to know what you really ought to mean and what you are justified in meaning by telling a story about the love of God for men and the eventual hope of men in God, then you must consider the pattern of the living and dying of Jesus. He is not mythological, whatever stories may have been part of the universe of discourse which made it possible to recognize him as the Christ and whatever stories a combination of faith, imagination and realistic insight may now encourage us to tell on the basis of the wholly unmythological and realistic happenedness of Jesus.

Thus the notion of the Messiah is decisively demythologized, finally taken out of the realm of story and imagination, and embodied in materiality and history in the happenedness of a person. This means that it is perfectly proper to drop the usage 'Jesus the Messiah' where Messiah/Christ remains a title, and go over to the usage 'Jesus Christ' where the whole phrase is a proper name, designating the person who is the historical vindication and expression of what the story of God's dealings with men is truly about. But the happenedness of the person who is Jesus Christ does not only demythologize the notion of Messiah; it also universalizes it. For Jesus Christ lived a life and worked out a vocation which was brought to suffering, death and forsakenness. Representatives of his own people rejected his teaching and ministry as not only mistaken but evil, his few disciples forsook him and fled, and he himself in his dying moments provided evidence that he was passing through a sense of being forsaken by the God upon whom his whole life was orientated. Thus all that made up the personalness of Jesus was effectively and experientially brought to nothing, reduced beyond absurdity to apparent non-existence.

The discovery that this Jesus was the Christ lay the other side of this, through the experienced discovery of his risenness, of his resurrection. Jesus, therefore, may have been brought to nothing but he was not reduced to nothing. Rather he was now known to be Jesus Christ, the expression of the Kingdom of God. Hence everything which had brought him to nothing was inevitably put under the most decisive question mark. Divine reality lay with Jesus, and everything which stood against Jesus stood against divine reality. All the restrictions which confined God's interest to a particular set of people, which confined the hope of salvation to the performance of a certain pattern of rules or shut up the hope of forgiveness within loyalty to a particular tradition—indeed, all the restrictions which suggested that love was confined only to those who were in a certain defined way lovable, were decisively challenged. God stood with Jesus against all such. This is a lesson which has never yet been completely learned, and a fact which has never yet had its full practical appreciation. It is an expression of the universal openness of Jesus Christ which is itself the expression of the universal openness of the God who is transcendentally personal and loving, of which I shall seek to say more in the last lecture. But, although we may fall short of appreciating the implications of the fact and much further short of responding to the living applications of the fact, it remains clear that the actuality of the life of Jesus Christ declares the completely universal concern of God over against the restrictive and partial concerns of men, not least men of religion.

The way in which this universality of Jesus Christ, which is a declaration of the universal concern of God, was actually worked out is, of course, of decisive importance with regard to our concern for persons. I have been maintaining, I think with some reason, that we do not need to lose faith in the possibilities of personalness and that we are right to see in the observable realities and potentialities of human personalness a significant clue to the underlying reality of things. But in setting out my grounds for optimism I have so far largely avoided consideration of what, for many, is the most effective ground of pessimism. I refer to those experiences which men cannot but regard as unmitigated suffering and inexplicable evil. We are the subject of happenings some of which are so randomly ruthless in their effects on particular human beings and groups of human beings that we are inclined to think that the most, but cold, comfort that we can get is to judge that the happenings are *so* random, so meaningless and inexplicable, that we may at least conclude that it is nonsense to think of them as ruthless. They are just meaningless and evidence of meaninglessness. However, they do count most powerfully against any belief that there is a purpose and pattern behind, in and beyond the universe which is truly to be thought of as personal and concerned with persons.

I have little doubt that it is in the observable occurrence of meaningless evil and destructive suffering that there lies the most potent threat to the sustaining of any ultimate faith in the fitting together of men and the universe of which they are part in a manner which fulfils man. It is often alleged that the dimensions and complexities of the universe as they are becoming known to us through the investigation of science make it unthinkable that such a universe could be truly related to a transcendent concern which has at least one of its foci in a concern for the fulfilment of the humanness of men. But the allegation that the size of the universe makes it necessarily clear that it can have no ultimate personal significance is simply a mistake. This mistake has two forms, which lock into and reinforce one another. The first form is the logical muddle which confuses size with significance. It is the human mind which has the capacity to discover vastness and to analyze microscopic minuteness. There is no logic which forces this mind to derive from these discoveries and analyses which are its own work that which is destructive of its own significance. Scale, large or small, is a personally neutral feature of the universe.

This *logical* muddle, or rather the muddled belief that there is a compelling connection between size and significance, is reinforced by the *psychological* confusion which projects on to the vastness and complexity of the universe our own personal sense of aloneness. It is not size which deprives one of the awareness of personalness or of the hope of discovering personal purposes and patterns. It is the failure to make or develop truly personal relationships in the context of one's own life. Personal lostness and the depair of all hope of personal fulfilment do not derive from the restriction or expansion of the horizons of observation and investigation but from the inability to form reciprocal relationships with our neighbours. Love truly experienced and truly reciprocated can teach us to look confidently for personal possibilities and personal fulfilment over limitless space and time and through an infinitude of microscopic divisions.

But the question is whether love is to be found anywhere else than in man, and whether the love which man begins to know has any reflection in the universe as a whole or in any way underlies that universe. To this question the fiercely contra-personal and strictly contra-purposive aspects of evil encourage a negative answer which is not to be turned aside by the clarity of logic or by coming to terms with our psychological condition. Human experience is that there are aspects of the materiality and historicity of the universe which are not only indifferent to love but which are experienced as lying wholly against the grain of any pattern which men can recognizably relate to a pattern of love. How dare we therefore continue to maintain that the human and personal reality of man has any hope of finding response and fulfilment in and through the reality of the universe and the reality which underlies and goes beyond that universe?

We dare to do so because the intuitions and hopes which arise from our admittedly imperfect experience of being persons and from our admittedly imperfect knowledge of the achievements and possibilities of love are confronted with the discovery that the Logos of the cosmos is embodied in the personal actuality of Jesus Christ. The shape of this actuality was one of suffering, dying and forsakenness. The personalness of Jesus Christ was brought to nothing. The pattern which gives shape to the universe, the Logos which expresses the purpose and pattern of the transcendent and personal God, is lived out in materiality and history as a man who succumbs to suffering and evil. It is only beyond this involvement and identification to the point of submission to nothingness that there emerges the discovery of resurrection, of triumphant newness, of the vindication of the suffering and destroyed humanity of Jesus as the pattern of the power of the Kingdom of God. We do not see how the purposes of love can be reconciled with the purposelessness of evil, but we do see that the human being who embodies the pattern of the loving God is both submerged in the destructiveness of evil and emerges from it as a distinctive, living and personal activity. The Logos of the cosmos is not a mythological theory but a crucified man. The hope of personal sense and fulfilment lies neither in ignoring evil nor in explaining evil, but in the fact that Jesus Christ endured evil and emerged from evil.

It will be necessary in the final lecture to make some attempt at the temerarious task of speaking of the consequent revelation that we have here of the suffering of God. Here we are concerned with the reality of man. In Jesus Christ we have the demonstration that the true, human and personal reality of man is not submerged, defined nor ended by what I can only call the inexplicable and present reality of evil. The shape of the givenness of Jesus Christ is a shape which takes in the effect and fact of evil and yet emerges with human personalness intact. Thus we have grounds in the givenness of materiality and history for giving full rein to our belief and hope that the emergence and fulfilment of human personalness is at the heart of the personal purpose which underlies, and is at work in, materiality and history.

It may be that a fully Christian faith and understanding would be, or will be, able to go on to perceive that what I have characterized as 'meaningless evil' is not meaningless, i.e. does not counteract but in fact works with the grain of that pattern of things which leads to the fulfilment of persons. Indeed, this may be the plain implication of my own argument. I have been arguing that the things concerning Jesus show us that we are right to perceive a purpose at work which brings out of the stuff of materiality and history the pattern of personalness and, in the end, the fulfilment of persons. Now, just as this stuff of materiality and history produces, or is led to produce, what we recognize as persons, so it produces what strikes us as meaningless evil. If Jesus Christ really is the Logos of the cosmos, then must we not see the cosmos as a homogeneous and developing whole which, as whole, tends towards the development and fulfilment of persons? The interaction of fundamental particles according to the laws of probability or whatever it is that is to be considered as the basic 'stuff' of physical reality is that which produces both persons and the 'meaningless evil' which arises for them out of other physical features like earthquakes, cancer and so on. Since we have grounds, in the reality of Jesus Christ and in the reality of persons, for holding that the processes are both patient of and productive of personal purposes, and also will be led to the fulfilment of personal purposes, then we must conclude that the processes are not meaningless and, therefore, that what strikes us as meaningless evil cannot be so.

As I say, I am inclined to believe that a fully Christian understanding of things (i.e. an understanding that was in full accordance with the reality of Jesus Christ) would develop in this direction.

Indeed some such development is probably demanded if we are to avoid dualism—the absurd understanding of the ultimate existence of two sorts of reality one of which is personally good and the other of which is intrinsically evil. However, I do not have a fully Christian understanding. I am at present trying to follow the argument wherever it leads, while very well aware that one can be only at a certain stage of this sort of argument with views about its ultimate direction and a varied assortment of loose ends, some stimulating, some frustrating and some frightening. In practice it seems sufficiently clearly the human lot to encounter and suffer from much that goes against the grain of humanity and personalness. As such, we experience it as meaningless evil and we have to see what the things concerning Jesus have to say to this situation. We may, I am sure, believe and hope that there is much more to be said than we have yet discerned, but we cannot effectively push the logic of the argument we believe we discern beyond what we find existentially and psychologically acceptable. For myself, therefore, I am clear that Jesus Christ enables us humanly and hopefully to face evil. I do not yet see that he enables us to explain evil.

But Jesus Christ is not only the demonstration of the ultimate possibility of the emergence and fulfilment of personalness, he is also the definition of the nature of personalness. It is in and through the givenness of the man Jesus Christ that we can at last give some precise outline to the notion of personalness which I have so far been making play the ambiguous rôle of a given which is both decisive and yet undefined. The personalness to be outlined is that which is to be seen in or hoped for in human beings. What may be said about the personalness of God must be considered in the next and last lecture.

Jesus Christ shows that a truly human person, a real man, is an individual who is wholly and consistently open to all the possibilities of materiality and history as they impinge upon him, to all the demands and possibilities of other persons as he encounters them, and to the reality of God which is both involved in materiality, historicity and other persons and also exists independently and transcendentally. Such a real man has never yet existed save in the defining case of Jesus Christ, but this is the reality of which all men to some extent partake, for which all men are destined and in which all men will find the complete fulfilment of their existence. It is human 'nature', all that is involved in being a man. But this nature is not something static, substantial, fixed. Rather it is an emergent and emerging pattern. The possibility of this pattern emerging and obtaining fulfilment out of the impersonal processes and patterns of the material universe and out of the events of history, patterned, patternless or destructive, lies in the antecedent fact of the transcendent and independent existence of the personal God and the consequent fact of the union of derived and emergent personalness with the divine personalness. The evidence for this understanding of the emerging process and final pattern of human personalness is focused on Jesus Christ, but supporting evidence is to be obtained from all those features of human existence which on reasonable investigation support the case for finding anthropology opening into theology.

The reality of man is to be understood in the light of the fact that the universe as created, that is, known in relation to the transcendent God, is material for purposive and personal living. Both history and matter can be *ordered* by human understanding, action and reaction to produce purpose and life which derives from humanness and enhances humanness. This is something which was uniquely discovered by the prophetic insight of inspired Israelites and Jews. Jeremiah and others, for example, discovered that the inner purpose and reality of history was to be perceived not in the destruction of Jerusalem but in the re-birth of the Jewish community. Creative human possibilities arise out of inhuman and chaotic happenings because there is always the possibility of response to the God who transcends every happening as well as every thing.

This prophetic insight was a God-given discernment of the way in which God's purposes of personal fulfilment are to be produced out of the stuff of materiality and history by the response of men to God. This response is a real and creative one made on the basis of God's initiative, sustained by God's creative presence, and consummated by God's decisive fulfilment. This way of God's working is recognized as men learn that there is a power other than the powers of the material processes which produce things and the historical interactions which produce events. This power, as far as men are concerned, is discernible in and through things and happenings but it is not the power of the things and happenings themselves, and it sets men free to overcome and transcend the impersonal forces of the things and happenings so that personal purposes and possibilities can be woven out of what is basically impersonal and even, apparently, contra-personal.

This crucial matter requires much more extended treatment than I can give it here but I may, perhaps, pause briefly on the one illustration I have mentioned. Is there any decisive factor which essentially differentiates the destruction of Jerusalem by the Babylonians from any overthrow of an independent small state by a neighbouring empire whether it be, say, in the Middle East, Far East or South America? Surely the answer as far as the materiality and historicity of the event goes must be 'No'. Famine, fear, bereavement, enslavement and exile have the same physical features everywhere and expansion and conquest are common historical phenomena. These features and phenomena present everywhere the same obliterating threats to humanness and the life of individuals as well as manifesting the same 'laws' both of materiality and of history. But in the case of the fall of Jerusalem, the involvement and response of such men as Jeremiah, Ezekiel and the author or authors of passages in the book of Isaiah now critically referred to as 'deutero-Isaiah', produced a unique discernment in, and interpretation of, the happenings which had perceptible consequences.

They saw in the events which led up to, constituted, and followed from the destruction of Jerusalem the hand and purpose of God. Thus the central and decisive happening was not the physical sequence of siege, famine, assault, death and exile, real and harrowing as it was. Nor was it the successful expansion of Nebuchadnezzar's Babylonian empire, historically real and influential as this was. Rather the central and decisive happening was the judgement of God upon his faithless people. Because of this, there did not occur that disappearance of the people who believed in their covenanted relation to the true and the living God which would have falsified the truth-claim implied in their belief. Rather, through and beyond the destruction and exile which was discerned as containing the judgement of God, there came the emergence of the Kingdom of Judah re-born as the people of the Jews, ready for the next stages of the encounter with, discernment of, and response to the true and living God.

The prophetic insight and inspiration was so to read God's purpose into materiality and history that it became possible to produce God's purpose out of materiality and history. But both the prophetic insight and the personal possibility depend primarily on the antecedent existence of the God who has personal purposes for materiality and history, and on the consequent fact that materiality and history thus lie available for personal ordering where there is responsive and responsible co-operation between God and man. By this co-operation between man and God, the possibilities of development into personal purposes which lie latent in the stuff of materiality and history because that stuff is basically 'created' actually emerge and are recognized by those persons who are themselves being formed by and yet emerging out of this same stuff. Thus men both are emergent persons and are the agents of emergent personal purposes. By discerning what is partially and potentially present, they have the opportunity to assist in its creative realization.

The persons who were led to give a clear expression to this vital clue to the pattern and possibilities of the universe in which men live, from which men emerge, and of which they are a homogeneous but potentially transcendent part, were the inspired prophets of the people who became the Jews. Their insight emerged within history and made its contribution to history. This contribution is not yet fulfilled, both in the sense that history is not yet fulfilled and in the sense that men have not yet seen all that is implied by and results from this contribution. To follow in the logic and in the power of the prophetic discernment demands a continuing openness to new understandings and new responses learnt from the present realities of materiality and history, an openness and discernment corresponding to that of the prophets themselves.

One type of openness and discernment which today corresponds in at least one vital respect to that of the prophets is that shown in the valid practice of science. There is a close and non-accidental analogy between the prophetic insight of which I have been speaking and the way in which science gives order to materiality. In practice, science and its consequent technology has led to a vast increase in the ability of men to order materiality for purposes of personal living. Here again (cf. Lecture VI, p. 61) it is not a question of claiming that the prophetic insight as historically expressed leads through the historical expressions of Christianity to the causal developments of science and technology. Rather it is to point out that science and technology now provide a vast extension of practical evidence that the stuff of the universe is patient of ordering by persons for personal purposes. In this, I am arguing, we are to see a further and, until it occurred, undreamed-of vindication of the prophetic insight that history and matter can be ordered by human understanding for humanness.

But the pattern of the development of personalness is the pattern of response to personalness. Unless man develops his derived personal reality in response to the underived personal reality of God, he loses his personalness in the impersonalness of the dependent materiality and history out of which he is emerging and in which he is either growing towards personalness or losing the chance of personalness. The pattern and purpose which encourages and fulfils personalness must transcend the processes of materiality and the pattern of history or it is their fragmentariness, unfinishedness and impersonalness which must be determinative. Jesus Christ, however, makes it clear that the last word and the ultimate hope lies with the emergent pattern of personalness, because these immanent developments are the intimate concern of the transcendentally personal. So we are to see the reality of man in the light of the direction in which he is developing, a direction of ever increasing possibilities of freedom, openness, and involvement with the potentialities both of the universe at large and of human beings among themselves. But this reality is both a developing reality and a dependent reality, developing from and dependent on materiality and history on the one hand, and dependent for fulfilment on development towards God on the other. There is no dichotomy between these two types of dependence and development, but there is a distinction, and if man fails to distinguish God from everything else then he loses his practical understanding of the true reality of everything else and of himself with it.

Personalness, therefore, is the self-conscious, open and characteristically human pattern which is to be found potentially and in varying degrees of development in each individual of the human species. This pattern has emerged out of the processes and patterns of the universe, and has the unique distinction of being both wholly rooted in the stuff of the universe and of reaching out beyond it. In the developing patterns of personalness the processes and patterns of the universe take on meaning and purpose. Further, what personalness itself requires for fulfilment is a fulfilling pattern and purpose. This fulfilment lies in the original and final transcendent personalness who is God. You cannot define the reality of man, the human person, without taking into account the reality of God.

But Jesus Christ makes it clear that this way of understanding the world, man and God is not anthropomorphism. It is true that man has always tended to see God in his (i.e. man's) own image. But God has not allowed man to rest in any idolatry, partial theism or false atheism, for God cares for man and will not leave him to the mercy of any impersonal forces, least of all those active in himself. Thus, in Jesus Christ, we are finally confronted with God taking on man's own, true and real image. In this historical presentation of the one fully real man we are confronted with the reality of the one true God. We have, therefore, to consider in the last lecture how we are finally and decisively prevented from thinking of God in our own image because God has finally and decisively made the human image his own.

VIII

True God

JESUS CHRIST IS the reality of man who confronts us with the reality of God. That is to say, firstly, that the historical person whose name was Jesus and who is now rightly designated Jesus Christ lived a life which brought to actual concrete expression in terms of particular materiality and historicity all that is necessary for the development of a complete man. All that is involved in thus being a man is that one is a particular personal individual, homogeneous in origin with the rest of the stuff of the universe, who emerges out of that stuff into the possibility of personalness through the particularity of the materiality and historicity of ones own origin and circumstances. The developing personal pattern who is a man has to mature and fulfil his particular personalness in openness to all surrounding materiality, historicity and personality. To bring all that is involved in being a man to the fulfilled possibilities of being a person in this way, it is necessary to be wholly open to the transcendent personalness of God, who is to be known both in and through all the surrounding circumstances and in himself. Thus Jesus Christ is all that is involved in being a man in that he emerges as every man must emerge and is involved as every man must be involved, and also in that the pattern of his living both is and achieves the perfect integration of his personalness in and through his perfect union with God.

In this matter of perfect integration of self and perfect union with God, Jesus Christ is all that is involved in being a man in the sense that he achieves, and is, all that it is necessary for a man to become if he is to achieve the fulfilment of the reality of his human personalness. Thus he is literally the one true man in the sense that he is the one so far existent example of what man must come to if he is to fulfil his humanness, and of what man will come to because God is concerned to achieve that fulfilment. In this way Jesus Christ is 'perfect in manhood', complete in his human nature, all that is involved in being a man. He is different from all other men only in the sense that he is the fulfilled achievement of that process and pattern which constitutes, in its various individualizations, the distinctive human existence of every man and in the case of every other man, that fulfilment which is yet to come.

It is in this sense of providing the historical example of the actualization and fulfilment of that pattern which is the pattern which will give fulfilment to every human being, that Jesus Christ may be said to be 'perfect in manhood' or to 'have human nature'. The 'nature' language is to be retained as standing for the distinctive and defining pattern which makes up and completes a fulfilled human person—all that is eventually and ultimately involved in being a man.

He is the living dynamic pattern and process which defines and constitutes his own person in the fulfilling way which every personal individuality must achieve if he or she is to be fulfilled. To point towards the completion of the picture it is highly significant and necessary to notice that the Christian hope is that the pattern of the one perfect man will be shared by all men so that in the end humanity as a whole will have its fulfilment 'in Christ'. But within the compass of the argument of these particular lectures there is no space to pursue the practical, social and splendid implications of this for our understanding of what it is, what it can be and what it will be to be a man in relation to every man and to God. We must rest with our statement that Jesus Christ is all that is involved in being a man, demonstrates and defines the nature all men share in, are developing and need to have fulfilled. (But see slightly further the postscript pp. 161 f.)

Secondly, this truly real man confronts us with the reality of God. As I have said, divine reality lay with Jesus. The Resurrection vindicated all that Jesus stood for in relation to the Kingdom of God. His livingness on the other side of his death made it clear that his original livingness represented the way God does things under the conditions of materiality and history in order to draw out of materiality and history his transcendent and personal purposes. Thus it becomes clear that the shape of the personalness of Jesus Christ is the embodied shape of the pattern of the personalness of God. The human Jesus Christ is what the divine God does, and what God does is to express himself as the man Jesus Christ in the conditions of materiality and history so that his purposes for materiality and history can be realized. As I have already said (Lecture V, p. 55), in Jesus Christ there is discovered the personal fulfilment both of God and of man.

But when we say that Jesus Christ is the personal fulfilment of man we mean something different from what we mean when we say that he is the personal fulfilment of God, although we are using both phrases correctly and fully of one and the same person, i.e. of Jesus Christ himself. This is so because God and man are distinct realities who, in and as Jesus Christ, are in perfect union. We are discussing here the Chalcedonian 'shape', viz. two distinct and perfect natures in perfect personal union.

The nature of man is to be an individual who, in a series of relationships, is a developing personal pattern recognizable as a dynamic continuation of a process of emergence and growth. Thus the personal fulfilment of man is when the individual personal pattern reaches a mature wholeness which finds fulfilment in the full expression and enjoyment of personalness in relation to the transcendent and inexhaustible personalness of God. Jesus Christ is the personal fulfilment of man in the sense that he achieved, expressed and enjoyed that full expression of personalness under conditions of materiality and history. Before Jesus Christ the fulfilment of man had never been achieved, and he is the fulfilment into which all men have the opportunity of entering.

The nature of God is to be God and we have to be very careful about saying anything more. But we may combine the whole teaching of the experience underlying the Bible about the unchangeable reliability of God with what we have discovered about the loss of the possibilities of personalness if they are found only in process and change, to reiterate from the whole theistic tradition that it is the nature of God to transcend all change and process and to be steadfast and complete in his being as God, free from any need of, or danger of, change. Thus to speak of the personal fulfilment of God is not to be saying that God has for the first time come into the possession and enjoyment of the full potentialities of his nature. It is to say that God has for the first time achieved under the conditions of materiality and history that full expression of the pattern of his personal purposes which expresses that in his nature which relates him to the whole cosmic process. We have God expressing his true and eternal self in the form which is appropriate to the conditions provided by the dependent and developing universe. Man has to achieve his fullness as man. God is always his fullness as God, but he does set himself to achieve his expression of this fullness in the midst of the processes and happenings of the universe in relation to the fulfilment of the purposes which spring from his fullness.

We have to set ourselves to consider the implications of the discovered fact that the human being who is Jesus Christ is the appropriate expression of the reality of God and see what effect this has on our understanding of the reality of God. We must, of course, be quite clear that there is one very important sense in which we cannot understand the reality of God. We cannot understand all that is involved in his being God, nor can we expect to understand, if I may so put it, why he is God or how he can succeed in being God. We must be content to accept the mystery of his being God because we have had kindled in us the faith and the awareness that he is God, that there is open to us the possibility of a reciprocity of relationship with him who is beyond anything and everything with which we have to do, but who none the less is concerned to have to do with us. Because he is concerned to have to do with us there are offered to us ways of understanding his reality, both that he is and also what is the true significance of his existence as far as we are concerned. But because it is God who has to do with us, we must be careful not to suppose that there is open to us an understanding of what might be called the structure of his nature and the articulation of his workings. In particular we must not imagine that we can expose, and satisfy ourselves about, the method or methods of his Incarnation.

Thus the position which I have tried to argue towards and set out, and which I believe to be required by the Christian understanding of the things concerning Jesus is as follows. We may know that Jesus is the Christ. We may also know that Jesus Christ is the historical presentation of the pattern, power and purpose of God. We of course know that Jesus Christ is human and that he is one person, himself and not someone else. We further know that God is God and, as such, distinct from everything else. To hold all this together we are obliged to say that Jesus Christ, as the person he is, is the personal union of God and man, the perfection of union of two distinct perfections. We are not called upon to explain *how* this can be so before we can maintain it, because we are not in a position to start from some theory about God and theory about man which will give us the clues and grounds for such an explanation. We are not theorizing at all. We are responding to recognizable givenness. Now we have to see what this givenness implies, how we are thereby required to understand the reality of man and the truth about God as far as understanding is open to us.

What then are we to understand about the reality of God in the light of the discovery that the human being who is Jesus Christ is the historically appropriate expression of this reality? Above all, surely, that the expression 'God is love' is no mere manner of speaking nor simply the sincere expression of a pious hope. The pattern of the personalness of the real man and the pattern of the personalness of the true God perfectly coincide, for Jesus Christ is the one integrated person who, in his historical actuality, is constituted by and as these patterns. Jesus Christ is one person, one integrated personality, one pattern of personalness. But this pattern is the pattern of the real man and the pattern of the true God, that is to say it is both human nature and divine nature. But God as transcendent and independent is necessarily distinct from man as emergent and dependent, as far as nature or defining reality goes. Nevertheless in Jesus Christ we have a real person, one pattern of personalness. It would seem, therefore, as I have just said, that in Jesus Christ the personal pattern of man and the personal pattern of God coincide.

But on reflection this suggestion, this attempted unfolding of the insight of faith, does not begin to be adequate to the reality presented to us. An integrated personality is not the coincidence of two patterns of personalness. An integrated personality is the fulfilled and fulfilling expression of one pattern of personalness. We can, however, I believe, begin to have some insight into the mystery which is the reality of one integrated personality, one fulfilled pattern of personalness, being the full personal expression of two patterns of personalness. This is the mystery of love. It is *not* the mystification arising from loose talk about love. Still less is it the muddle arising from romantic escapism indulging in fantasies about love. We are concerned with the concrete presentation of the mystery which is love in action, seen in its fullness in the embodiment of God as the crucified man, Jesus Christ, and experienced in its beginnings, at its fringes as we might say, by every human being who has begun to share his or her essential personal reality with another in the first faltering steps of the interchange of love.

As I think I might perhaps be beginning to understand it, I glimpse somewhat as follows. Jesus Christ is the purposive and personal pattern of God and man in union. The shape of the personalness of his human life was the obedience and service of love, love which is, and which comes from, full openness to God and full openness to one's neighbour. Real man is in existence when there is perfect, freely given, and therefore fully personal, obedience to the two commandments of loving God with the whole of one's personality and of loving one's neighbour with the full openness with which a fully integrated personality is open to the realities of his or her own self. In such a fully personal and open expression of love the two commandments are fulfilled in such a way that they cease to be commandments, for such love is not in any way the result of, or related to, the pressure of an external command, but is the wholly spontaneous expression of the personality concerned. Thus in Jesus Christ as far as his humanity goes, we have the perfection of the obedience of love and of the service of love which is the perfect expression of the fulfilled and fulfilling pattern of human personalness. This is what men are 'for', and this is how they are to enjoy and fulfil being themselves, by being and expressing what they are for, namely the reciprocity of the openness of love.

But the full, fulfilled and fulfilling reciprocity of the openness of love is not to be found among men as yet. Where Jesus found it, and what enabled Jesus humanly to express it unwaveringly despite the lack of adequate human response, was in the openness of the love of God. The pattern of the human personalness of Jesus was determined by the obedience of love expressed in the service of love. This was perfectly matched by the pattern of the divine personalness which is transcendent love likewise expressed, in relation to materiality and history, as the service of love. If I may be allowed to strive after crude simplicity of expression for so high a matter, which if it is true, must be profoundly simple, I would say that what we are to learn is that when the love of God and the love of man really get down to it they come to the same thing. Or, rather, since love is so highly personal and personalness is so bound up with love, we should better say that when God who is truly love, and man who can find his true reality only in love, get down, in the stuff of materiality and history, to expressing their true selves, it comes to the same person. Thus Jesus Christ is the person who is the perfect coincidence of the pattern of personalness determined by the human service of love and that determined by the divine service of love. But because we are confronted with the coincidence of patterns of personalness which are determined and defined by love, we do not encounter coincidence but personal union. God *is* the loving man. The man *is* the loving God. There is through perfect love the perfect interchange of existence which is the height and depth of personal union. The existence of Jesus Christ depends wholly on the living God while the existence of Jesus Christ is expressed wholly as the loving man. We may not and we cannot divide the person, the personality or the personalness. But we may and we must understand that the personal union is a union of distinctness which depends for the very possibility of its existence on the initial, independent and transcendent existence of God who is personally and purposively concerned to unite emergent, dependent and fulfilled human personalness to himself.

Whatever may be made of this attempt of mine to make one more halting contribution to the contemplation of the mystery with which the givenness of Jesus confronts us, I feel bound to follow up certain ideas which it suggests concerning our proper and legitimate understanding of God. I am sure that we have now left the realms of incisive logical argument and I would myself judge that we are also very near, if not beyond, the limits of the realms of even tentative dogmatic definition. But I remain convinced that there is yet a realm wherein we may, with fear and trembling mingled with hope and joy, expect to be able to delineate certain perceptions which have some reasonable chance of being insights into the mystery of God in which men are called to partake.

Consider the conclusion, *à propos* of Jesus Christ, that God is the loving man, the man is the loving God. This makes it clear that it is perfectly possible for the reality of the transcendent God to be expressed as a function of, and in terms of, total involvement in the processes of materiality and the events of history. Doubtless we are to be clear that such a total involvement is possible only when materiality has reached the level of personalness, but at that level we are shown that there is no contradiction in actuality between the divine transcendence and immanence. No matter what theistic theories may have held to be the case, it is clear that in practice, that is in the practical exercise by God of his divine personalness in relation to the stuff out of which we emerge, there is no contradiction between transcendence and immanence, between being wholly other and being wholly involved, between being completely free of all necessary attachments to anything else and being completely committed to everything else. The absolute freedom of God, wherein he transcends and is detached from everything else, is no bar to his total involvement in and concern for all the personal possibilities of the universe because as he is absolutely free so he is absolutely love. It thus becomes quite clear that the tendency in much current theological debate to oppose transcendence to immanence or insist on substituting involvement language for all detachment language is simply a mistake arising out of a combination of misunderstanding and ignorance of the authentic implications of the authentic Christian tradition. It is a mistake too, as I hope I have shown in earlier lectures, which is destructive of man via the demotion of God. Transcendence without immanence makes nonsense of God, immanence without transcendence makes nonsense of man. Both are quite untrue to the givenness of Jesus Christ.

The givenness of the personalness of Jesus Christ is, then, the givenness of the personalness of God in terms of materiality and history. This presents us not only with the involvement of God in process and event, but also with the identification of God with the suffering man. The personal involvement which expresses the pattern of the personalness of the loving God leads to that expression of the divine which is the suffering and dying man. This is an extension of the mystery of the union of love which is certainly very hard to accept, let alone to begin to understand, but I believe it to be undeniable. God expresses himself as the man who suffers, is forsaken and dies.

Attempts have been made to explain, mitigate and, in effect, to deny this mystery by various uses of the concept of *kenosis*, of the notion of the emptying out of the divine in the Incarnation, to which there is some sort of reference in what is probably a very early Christian hymn made use of by Paul in the second chapter of his letter to the Philippians. These attempts, when they go beyond being poetic references or perceptive uses of language which attempt to pass on partial but sometimes penetrating insights, make it abundantly clear that the pursuit of detailed expositions of the method of the Incarnation or of the articulation of the divine and human in Jesus Christ are useless if they are not harmful. The language of emptying is already referring to the expression of the divine love in the historical reality of Jesus Christ, and cannot be used as if it enables us further to unpack that mystery. It does, however, help to point us, not to what lies behind and so makes possible the mystery, but to what the mystery actually shows us.

This is, as far as I can see it and put it, that God is perfectly willing, and therefore able, to give himself away in the furtherance of his purposes of love which are themselves the expression of the pattern of his personalness. The man Jesus Christ who is the embodiment of the pattern of the personalness of God is brought to nothing. He is not thereby reduced to nothing because he is the expression of the transcendent and omnipotent God. But this transcendent omnipotence is the power of absolute love which finds true expression in going out from the pattern of personalness wholly into and wholly for the other. This is not to give love away nor to empty out what it is to be divine, but rather to give expression to what it is to be divine, to be love. Hence the bringing to nothingness is not the

final reduction to nothingness but the completion of that identification which is the triumphant and free work of love whereby love
works forward to fulfilment at any costs and through any odds. In so
far as we can glimpse the true meaning and the true power of love, I
believe we can glimpse the possibility of the mystery that God
expresses himself as the suffering, forsaken and dying man. In
relation to the practical problem of evil, God is neither indifferent,
ncompetent nor defeated. He is involved, identified and inevitably
triumphant.

The involvement of the transcendent God in our stuff of materiality and history gives us hope. But the identification of God with the
suffering, dying and forsaken man must give us pause. I do not,
however, think that we may finally turn aside, however much we
may shrink, from attempting to face the fact that God suffers. The
embodiment of the pattern of personalness of God is the pattern of
the personalness of Jesus Christ. The reality of this latter pattern is
suffused with suffering. There can be no reality in the union of
pattern and personalness unless suffering has a real place in the
pattern of the personalness of God. The givenness of Jesus Christ
surely demands that we try to understand that the love of God is not
condescension but compassion. The question mark which evil suffering places upon the existence of man in the world and the whole
meaningful existence of the universe has superimposed upon it the
Cross, as the expression in materiality and history of God's real and
true openness to all the suffering which seems, as matter of observable but inexplicable facts, to be concomitant with the emergence
of his purposes. Since God suffers, and God is God, we are not left
with the absurdity wherein evil and suffering emerge as the indifferent randomness which destroys all meaning, nor are we left with a
perhaps even more terrifying and more nonsensical dualism in which
a divine goodness struggles in a precariously matched eternal conflict with a contradictory yet equally divine evil. Rather we are
confronted with the opportunity of faith in, and knowledge of, the
God who secures the hope of the fulfilment of derived personalness
by accepting, absorbing and transforming all that is contrary to it.

But the fact must be faced that to take this line is to invite an
atheistic retort which would have much support, although from a

different viewpoint, from within the theistic tradition. The retort is 'If God suffers, then surely he is not God'. The atheistic point of this retort is the conclusion that there is, after all, no God. The theistic point is the conclusion that in the last analysis God does not suffer. My own judgement would be that it might be nearer the mark to make the counter-retort 'Unless God suffers, there is no God'. For if God does not suffer, but produces his purposes out of suffering by a divine condescension proceeding from absolute detachment, then it is exceedingly difficult to see how he can be regarded as other than a cosmic monster. On the other hand, the notion that God has let himself in for involvement in suffering would seem to have its futility best thrown into relief by saying that such a notion justifies the wry and near blasphemous comment that God is a fool—and a cosmic fool at that. At any rate it is very clear that we have the whole notion of God at risk.

I see nowhere else to turn in all this than to the givenness of Jesus Christ, which is, no doubt, simply to say that I am a Christian. Here I see that, indeed, everything is at risk. The man whose givenness I see reason to understand as the embodied givenness of God passes through an experience which he interprets as God-forsakenness. I believe that this is to be seen as evidence that God enters into the experience of that in the universe which counts for atheism. Thereby it is shown that it need not so count but that it can be brought within the scope of the purposes of personalness and love. Thus we are confronted with a God in whom it is possible to believe when living in a world with the sort of materiality and history that is actually known to us. If, however, we conclude that God has taken too big a risk, we shall not believe in him. We shall, however, still be confronted with the givenness of Jesus and with the dimension of personalness.

Thus I cannot escape the conclusion that the true God, as he is seen through Jesus Christ, must be understood to be truly open to the suffering of the world. We are free, therefore, both to rest in his compassion and to be shaped by his compassion into a passionate attack on all that adds to suffering or stands in the way of its mitigation and transformation. Love is no idle word, the love of God is no idle force, and those who would wish to be counted as lovers of God can never rest content with indifferent or cowardly idleness. Moreover I do not believe that an understanding of the reality of the God who is love along the lines I am diffidently suggesting in fact runs counter to the authentic insight contained within the traditional theistic notion of the impassibility of God.

God, it has always been held by those who have understood and experienced believing in God as response to existent and authentic reality, does not change. He is not at the mercy of events and things for his existence as God nor for the enjoyment and expression of his essential reality as God. Whatever his relationship to continuing processes and developing patterns, he himself is not to be equated with those processes and patterns, and he is not dependent for his being God, or his being as God, in any way on the movements, developments, changes in materiality and history. This insight into the transcendent independence of God in his godness is, I am convinced, a valid one. The God who is nothing but involvement is not the God of biblical encounter nor the God of theistic worship nor the God who is required by, and the fulfilment of, the mystery of personalness and love. The God who is necessary to the fulfilment of the mystery of love cannot exist *because* he is this fulfilment, nor *in order to* be that fulfilment, nor *in so far as* that fulfilment comes into being. Rather, the possibility of love and personalness emerges, and the fulfilment of personalness and love is realistically to be looked for, because or in so far as God exists in his transcendental personalness antecedently to and independently of these possibilities. God does not exist in order to guarantee man fulfilment. Such a notion is idolatrous anthromorphism. Nor is authentic belief in the living God man's projection on to the universe of his unrealistic determination to hold, contrary to reality, that there is a possibility of his fulfilment. We are rapidly gaining sufficient psychological insights to dissipate that sort of fantasy and to enable us to move into a clarity in which it will emerge whether there is a true God or not. The true God exists because he is the true God and it is a *consequence* of his transcendentally independent existence both that man exists and that man has the hope of fulfilment as man.

God, therefore, depends only and wholly upon himself for the totality and fulfilment of his existence as God. This means that he must be understood as having no necessary relations with any thing or person other than himself. The relations are not necessary because God in no way depends on them for being God. But this has been usually taken to imply that if God does choose to establish relations with something other than himself then these relations can *make no difference to him.* If his being in relationship to the universe and to men makes a difference to God, then he either depends on the effect of these relations to enable him to become more truly God, or he succumbs to the effect of these relations by becoming less truly God. In either case he is then shown to be not God but simply a function of the universe. Hence the godness of God is held to require an understanding of his transcendent independence which excludes the possibility of any of his real relations with the universe and men making any difference to him, and this has been expressed as his impassibility, as his being out of the reach of all experience and suffering which could make any difference to or have any effect upon him.

In the light, however, of the experience of God which builds up to the recognition of Jesus Christ as the embodiment of the pattern of God's personalness, it would seem that we are required to interpret our understanding of what is involved in God's transcendent existence in a somewhat different way to that normally associated with the notion of impassibility. We have to build into our understanding of the godness of God the implications of the fact that we are confronted with evidence of God's practical capacity for involvement and identification. As I have felt obliged to suggest, this must produce the conclusion that God suffers. I would reiterate the suggestion that this is indeed so but that the suffering of God does not make any difference to his being God. For neither the Bible, nor Jesus Christ, nor our experience and understanding of what is involved in personalness, supports the notion that we are to conceive of the perfection of God, or of any personalness, as the perfect union of a set of static attributes which can, so to speak, be knocked off their pinnacles of perfection by something happening to them. Rather we have revealed to us something much more like a dynamically active pattern which is to be appreciated in terms of love and loving.

I would suggest that we can at least entertain the notion that fully personal love and fully loving personalness might be absolutely capable of being completely open to all the effects resulting from any relations whatever without this making any difference at all to the nature, pattern, purpose and effectiveness of this love. I would sum up the point I am trying to make here by saying that the notion of the impassibility of God stands for the fact that God is in no way dependent on anything outside himself for being himself, and that further, and most importantly, nothing whatever can put him off being God. He is the Lord and he does not change. But he has made it known to us that the energy which manifests the essence of his being, in so far as manifestation is possible, is the energy of love. His unchangeability, therefore, is unquenchable love which can and does suffer everything at a deeper level of fully personal experience than is either open to or endurable for any of us, but this makes not one iota of difference to the reality of this love. The experienced reality of the Cross has to be seen as pointing to the centre of what it means to God to be God, but this is no threat to his unchangeable and imperishable divinity. It is the very expression of it, whereby the power of his personalness is made overwhelmingly effective for all men without the individual personalness of any single man being thereby overwhelmed. For to be taken up by personal love which is expressed in terms of complete openness, identification and compassion to the point of irresistible union is not to be swallowed up but to be set free to be yourself, in union with God and with every other loved and loving self.

But, it may be urged, all this is only a vision, a possible perspective, a personal hope. So it is. But it is a vision which has strong claims to have elements of true insight arising from the givenness of Jesus Christ rooted in materiality and events, arising also from the observed givenness of personalness and renewed in the continually experienced givenness of the possibilities which arise out of and in connection with the worship of God. The vision is, however, always obscured when the worship is obscured. For it is in worship that one is faced with both the offer and the demand of transcendence, of the immeasurable distance which goes with the intimate closeness of the living God whose life is love. Worship is the way of experiencing the infinite openness of the possibilities of the personal. And this openness is, as far as we are concerned, the practice of the response of love to the love of the God who in the infinite openness of his love is endlessly and gloriously worshipful. There is no end to the possibilities of being human, but this openness is joy and hope, not weariness and despair, for the endless possibilities exist already in and as the glory of God.

But we shall never progress, indeed we shall scarcely begin, in the true worship of the true God which is the way to the fulfilment of man, unless we look for the grace to be truly scientific. Our investigation into the givenness of Jesus Christ has surely made one thing clear. To be human and personal is to be open to whatever is given, to all data. We are in the image of God, but this describes our potentialities more than our present realities. Thus we must not anthropomorphically think of God in *our* image. That is, we must not be trapped in any symbol, picture or definition of God. The *image* we have of God, still less the image we have of ourselves, is never decisively definitive of our commitment to our true reality, which is to be fulfilled in the reality of the transcendent and inexhaustible God. Similarly, no present theory of the universe must finally shut in our developing understanding of that universe, of our place within it, and of the reality of the God who is making us for himself in and through the stuff of that universe. The insight of the vision which Jesus Christ offers us will be lost unless we put into practice whatever insight we so far have by a continually open investigation of all that is presented to us and by a willingness to respond to every new imperative which such investigation throws up for us.

We are not sufficiently personal as yet to practice such openness by ourselves, but if we are to become fully and truly personal we need such openness for ourselves. Our hope lies in the evidence of Jesus Christ that the openness we need is offered to us by and as the openness of the love of God. We need be trapped in no mythology, no theory, and in no fragmentation of absurdity. We have, rather, the opportunity of hopeful openness in the fearless development of science and in the loving development of personalness. Both come together in the worship of the transcendent God and in dependence upon the immanent God.

Even if there has seemed to be some coherence and force in some part of my argument as I have tried to unfold it, you will still surely ask, 'But what does this mean?'. This is what you should ask and what we must always ask. If it is true that the fulfilment of our human personalness lies in union with the personalness of God, then we can never in this life suppose that we have reached the end of meaningfulness. Jesus Christ is a sufficient statement of our hope and definition of our direction. God will not let us go back on what has been said in him about the possibilities and fulfilment of love and personalness. But the meaning of the following of Jesus Christ does not now lie in resting in indicatives. It is to be discovered in the obedient response to imperatives and in the hopeful facing of questions.

POSTSCRIPT

The Question of Truth

I HAVE BEEN attempting to argue for the truth of Christianity in the sense that I have been seeking a reconsideration of the truth about God and about man which is implied by Jesus. I have not been attempting to show by argument 'that Christianity is true', whatever precisely would be meant by that phrase. I must hope that the lectures do reflect and convey my conviction that the things concerning Jesus are of central and decisive importance in putting us on to the realities of man's situation with regard to the world and God. Since I suffer from the further conviction that reality must be faced, I naturally believe and desire that others should see and be convinced of those realities about God and man which are demonstrated in Jesus and pointed to by Jesus. This desire of mine is reinforced by the evident fact that what is declared about reality by and through Jesus is realistic and practical good news about the possibilities and direction of human fulfilment. The things concerning Jesus constitute and imply a universal Gospel the contents of which are so humanly worthwhile that it would demonstrate the extreme of inhumanity not to wish urgently to share this good news. Hence I find myself under precisely the same command and obligation to 'preach the gospel' as did the Christians of New Testament times.

I do not believe, however, that the truth, even when it is good news which points towards a glory greater than we can so far comprehend, is something which can be forced upon people. Indeed, 'the truth as it is in Jesus' surely underlines this point. For he established the reality of his person, his mission and his message through identification and beyond death in a manner which displayed faith and love rather than enforced submission. The truth which concerns persons, if, as Jesus demonstrates, it is to do with the fulfilment of persons, must remain personal and free and cannot compel impersonal acquiescence. Moreover, seeing that this truth is to do with the fulfilment of the potentialities of men in the reality of God, it becomes clearer than ever that it is truth which cannot be established but must establish itself. God cannot be manipulated by or established upon lesser realities than himself.

Hence it is possible to argue for the truths involved in the things concerning Jesus only by looking to see what those truths are, investigating them and seeking to respond to them. Christian truth must be essentially experiential and experimental and always as much a hope as a possession. This is simply to say that 'Christians', i.e. those consciously concerned to respond to the things concerning Jesus, are by this very concern required to follow a way of authentic involvement with serial reality rather than to take refuge in what is believed to be a castle, but turns out to be a cage, of enforceable dogma. How, under such circumstances, does one respond to one's obligation to preach the gospel, and how can we hope that men and women may become effectively and experientially alerted to the living meaning and truth which must lie behind and beyond the investigations which I have been pursuing in these lectures, if there is any truth in them?

I have thought it necessary to add a postscript to the lectures about this question of the apprehension of truth because I dared to hope as I wrote them that they might engage with this matter of truth and the gospel as they are to be looked for, responded to and lived out. But as I delivered them I felt more and more that they were but the most preliminary survey of ground which had yet to be entered upon and lived in. I suppose it is the inevitable lot of anyone who believes himself to have an inescapable call to attempt to speak of the realities of God and man, to know always that he finishes rather far short of the point at which he ought really to begin. But this necessary reminder of the distance one is from apprehending and conveying that truth which seems none the less in some way to have got hold of one, served also to direct my attention to the essential rôle in the practice of the living discovery of truth of the community.

In these lectures on God and man in Jesus Christ I have found practically no space for any reference to, and certainly no opportunity for any discussion of, the communal dimension of personality and the fulfilment of personalness or of the communal dimension of Christian living and of the apprehension of the truth of the things concerning Jesus. I wish to register this here for two reasons, both connected with types of 'follow-up' which the experiment of these lectures would require if they are to lead in the direction of the practical apprehension and application of truth. That is, if we are to validly engage in an 'argument for the truth of Christianity'.

The first reason is that I do not believe that it is arguments and investigations of the type exemplified in these lectures which play the primary rôle either in persuading people to pay attention to the question 'What is truly involved in believing in Jesus Christ?' (see Preface, pp. vi f.) or in helping people to work out an answer to that question. People will be persuaded to take up this question only in so far as they come across groups of persons who are attempting to be believers in Jesus Christ and who are displaying a style of life and a manner of involvement in practical realities which are *prima facie* authentic, i.e. have something about them which invite further attention. On matters of fundamental importance, persons must gain a hearing for arguments. Christians, therefore, cannot hope to regain evangelistic effectiveness simply by renovating the terms or the types of their argument. We have to demonstrate authentic practice before we can hope for effective preaching. And this is entirely in the logic of the things concerning Jesus. Jesus was discovered to be the Word of God and the Logos of the cosmos in and through his personal embodied living. God makes himself known in human practice. Those who believe that it is in the following of Jesus that God is above all to be known and shown can scarcely expect to find any other effective way of learning for themselves or of gaining a hearing from others than the way of involvement and practice. So it is also that the meaning and truth of the arguments deployed in these lectures can only be discovered by those who are already sympathetic to the question about Jesus in so far as they are willing to throw in their lot with others in the practical pursuit of the human, the worshipful and the Christ-like in and in relation to that materiality and historicity with which they are individually and corporately involved. Thus unless the arguments of these lectures can be followed up by and tied in with corporate and individual experiments in attempted Christian practice, they can lead nowhere.

Secondly, I wish to draw attention to the bearing of this dimension of community on my other main question 'What is really involved in being a man?' (Preface, p. vii). Any serious answer to this question must clearly include consideration of that actual community which shapes a man and that to-be-hoped-for and striven-for community which enables that fulfilment of a man which interlocks with and contributes to the fulfilment of other men. Personalness has a communal dimension, and individuality neither emerges from, nor is to be fulfilled by, isolation. Hence the investigations of these lectures need to be followed up in relation to the social side of the life of men, and the things concerning Jesus need to be carefully scrutinized in relation to all those ways in which human togetherness is threatened, fails or never begins to be developed. We shall not be able to make satisfactory and effective sense of the cosmic significance of Jesus unless and until we develop and re-develop practical implications of the social significance of Jesus. The Kingdom of God stands for the fulfilment of the personal purposes of the universe in a perfected and a perfecting society. I do not myself see effective sense being made of the theological and anthropological realities of the things concerning Jesus without commitment to the social and political dimensions of men's living. Thus it becomes clearer than ever that the effective and life-enhancing things about the truth as it is in Jesus have been scarcely touched on in the lectures which might, at best, turn out to be a sort of intellectual girding up of the loins for a task which makes demands of the will and the emotions quite as much as of the intellect.

Theologically speaking, too, I have not only failed to move on to effective territory concerned with working out the truth about man. I have scarcely moved either into any effective discussion of the mystery of God. I have made no reference to or discussion of that articulation of the understanding of the mystery of God which emerges from the things concerning Jesus and which is symbolized by the doctrine of the Trinity. Such a discussion is very necessary if one is to follow up the present set of investigations in any effective way. For although the doctrine of the Trinity has been much theorized about and obscured by many theories it is, in essence, a non-theoretical distillation and articulation of the experience of the God and Father of Jesus Christ which came to men as they responded to the things concerning Jesus in the power of the continuing presence of his Spirit. As such, the doctrine of the Trinity points to many avenues of investigation which can throw some light on the reality of the transcendentally personal God in his relations with the derived personalities whose ultimate hope and fulfilment he is. In particular, I am sure that the reality to which the symbol of the Trinity points is highly relevant to that balance of the individual, the relational and the communal in which the fulfilment of personalness may be looked for.

Thus, if these lectures have any value or significance it will be only as they are a preface and pointer to a continuing programme of investigation and commitment. The end of the argument in which these lectures join will come, I believe, only when we are brought to that perfected community which is the fulfilment of humanness through Jesus Christ in the reality of God himself. Only then may we hope to know for certain both what the truth truly is and that such truth truly exists. Meanwhile, I suggest that in living by faith we are, in fact, arguing for and searching for truth. The peculiar nature of the faith which is response to the reality in Jesus Christ is the assurance that the truth for which we seek has already sought and found us. The peculiar danger of faith is to pervert this assurance into a self-centred conviction that we have found the truth. So we can seek because we have been found and are ourselves committed to putting whatever we find at the service of and to the test of further seeking. This is the experiment which is living .And I suspect that what the argument of these lectures comes to is the case for maintaining that the only experiment which gives room enough for truly human living is the experiment into God. Further, this is the experiment which is both possible and has every hope of a successful outcome because a proper understanding of the things concerning Jesus gives us reason to believe that God has undertaken the experiment of being a man.

POSTSCRIPT NOTE

Since the publication of these Bampton Lectures, I have taken up
the discussion of the doctrine of the Trinity in *The Contradiction
of Christianity* (especially chapter 10), SCM Press 1976.